The Science of Managing Our Digital Stuff

The Science of Managing Our Digital Stuff

Ofer Bergman and Steve Whittaker

The MIT Press
Cambridge, Massachusetts
London, England

This book was set in Stone Sans and Stone Serif by Toppan Best-set Premedia Limited. Printed and bound in the United States of America.

Library of Congress Cataloging-in-Publication Data

Names: Bergman, Ofer, author. | Whittaker, Steve, 1957- author.
Title: The science of managing our digital stuff / Ofer Bergman and
    Steve Whittaker.
Description: Cambridge, MA : MIT Press, [2016] | Includes
    bibliographical references and index.
Identifiers: LCCN 2016015017 | ISBN 9780262035170 (hardcover : alk.
    paper)
Subjects: LCSH: Personal information management.
Classification: LCC HD30.2 .B4647 2016 | DDC 650.1--dc23 LC record
available at https://lccn.loc.gov/2016015017

10   9   8   7   6   5   4   3   2   1

To my wife, Rutu, and our children, Michali and Hillel
Ofer

To my wife, Lyn, and our children, Ewan and Isabel, and to my
mother, Julie, and my sisters, Chris and Sue
Steve

Contents

Acknowledgments

We would like to thank our participants and research partners in the many studies reported in this book; Professor Rafi Nachmias and Professor Ruth Beyth-Marom for their help in developing the user-subjective approach; and Google, for granting us two Google Faculty Awards.

Introduction

Personal information management (PIM) is an activity in which an individual stores personal information items in order to retrieve them later. PIM can be performed in a physical environment (e.g., an office), using mobile devices (e.g., mobile phones and tablets), or via personal computers. On personal computers, information items include documents, email, web favorites, tasks, and contacts. Despite the fact that PIM is a fundamental aspect of computer-based activity and that millions of computer users manage their personal information several times a day, there is surprisingly little research on the subject. However, in recent years, the topic has attracted increasing scientific attention.

For almost two decades, this book's authors have been conducting pioneering research to shed light on PIM behavior and system design. We started working separately, but since 2007 we have worked mostly together. Altogether, we have published over forty PIM papers, ten of which are coauthored. We see each of our studies as a piece in a larger puzzle. This book puts these pieces together, presenting a bigger picture of PIM. Our main focus is on presenting the picture emerging from our own research. We do not intend to provide an exhaustive review of the entire PIM field.

The theme of this book is that PIM is fundamentally different from other types of information management, and our aim is to provide a scientific foundation for this new field. All three parts of the book address this:

In part I, we argue that the emphasis of modern information theories is misplaced due to focusing exclusively on information discovery in public data. We draw attention to the importance of personal data and suggest curation as an alternative model for PIM. We define a three-stage model for curation— keeping, management, and exploitation—and review existing literature, focusing on our own studies regarding each of these stages.

Part II demonstrates that technologies that work well for other information management fields fail for PIM. We examine the hierarchical folder method that currently dominates PIM and compare it with three proposed alternatives: search everything, tag everything, and group organization. We describe multiple studies showing that these alternative methods that work well on the web have little uptake for PIM, with users preferring to manually organize and navigate to personal data. We conclude by presenting research that explains the underlying cognitive and neurological reasons for this strong preference for folder navigation.

This demonstration that PIM is indeed a different sort of game means that we need specific PIM principles for building successful systems. In part III, we introduce the user-subjective approach to PIM system design. The user-subjective approach exploits the fact that in PIM, the person who organizes the information is the same person who later retrieves it. This approach

suggests that PIM systems should exploit subjective (user-dependent) attributes in their design. We propose design principles
that exploit subjective attributes and describe concrete designs
that implement those principles. Many of these designs have
been deployed and positively evaluated, offering support for the
utility of the user-subjective approach.

We conclude the book by outlining future challenges for the
field of PIM.

I   Personal Information Management: The Curation Perspective

Each of us now has a large collection of personal digital data, including personally created documents, spreadsheets, and presentations, as well as photos we have taken. In addition to this self-created information, our personal collections also include the countless emails, messages, and texts that we have sent and received, many documents or photos shared by others, and other public resources (such as maps or web pages) that we have accessed from the Internet. What unifies this disparate data into a personal collection is that we judge that it may be valuable to us in the future. We therefore seek to preserve and actively organize this data ourselves because we want to ensure access to it at some future time.

This book provides a scientific understanding of how we select, organize, and access such personal collections. *Personal information management* (PIM) is the process by which individuals curate their personal data in order to reaccess that data later. Curation involves three distinct processes: how we make decisions about what personal information to keep, how we organize that kept data, and the strategies by which we access it later. As noted in the introduction, this book's authors have been researching this topic for almost twenty years, resulting in multiple publications. What we write here will be focused mainly on our own research. We view PIM through the lens of our own theoretical viewpoint and data, although we will refer to the work of others where relevant.

PIM has not received much attention historically. One reason for this lack of attention is that, until recently, people's personal digital collections usually were quite small. More importantly, theorizing within information and computer science has been concerned with the organization and retrieval of *public* data. Information management theory typically has explored how information professionals (such as librarians or database designers) structure public data to promote access. Such theory has developed reliable organizational methods to facilitate retrieval of this public information, using objective properties of data or consensual categorization schemes such as the Dewey decimal system. It also has studied processes by which end users explore and retrieve information from such public archives. Computer science theory too has focused on public collections, but has taken a different approach. Innovations in computer science include techniques to automatically index large online public collections, allowing user access via keyword search.

PIM is different. Rather than developing theory and methods about how people access public collections, PIM curation focuses on how individual users select, organize, and access their *personal* collections. We will see that personal collections are organized differently. In the next chapter, we characterize the curation process in PIM as a conversation that we have with our future selves. Following that metaphor, in PIM, each user exploits subjective properties of their personal data for organization, capitalizing on the fact that the organizer and retriever are the same person. Knowing that I am organizing for my future self allows me to harness organizational schemes that would not be understood by others and that may reflect specific interactions that I have had personally with my information.

Chapter 1 provides motivation for an increased scientific understanding of personal information curation. We first argue why curation is a critical information management problem. We elaborate on exactly how curation differs from other approaches to information management, which are focused on discovering and consuming new public information. We further detail the need for improved understanding of curation by characterizing the complexity and extent of personal archives. We introduce the curation life cycle, outlining the different processes of keeping, management, and exploitation that are involved in information curation. We then describe important properties of personal information—such as action/information orientation, accumulation status, and uniqueness—that have important implications for these curation processes. Chapters 2–4 summarize research on the curation processes of keeping, management, and exploitation.

1 Personal Archives and Curation Processes

Not Consumers, but Curators

This book is about humans and their relation to information. A defining characteristic of the technology revolution of the last twenty years has been increased availability of information. We now have ready access to an astonishing array of information—such as maps, encyclopedias, news, medical information, and social media—that was unavailable even a few years ago. This has led to a great deal of theorizing within the computer and information management communities, advancing a particular view of humans and how they use information. According to these theories, people are like explorers, constantly seeking out and consuming new information from public collections. This book will argue that this prevailing view of humans as consumers of novel public information is insufficient. In particular, we will argue that this consumer view ignores many pressing problems of information management that concern how we keep, organize, and reuse our personal information. Of course, we are all interested in the latest political news, sports scores, or even celebrity gossip, and we may possibly even want to know about new medical or technical developments—but this focus on novelty overlooks a fundamental aspect of how we experience and use information.

The current exclusive focus on seeking out novel public information ignores visceral concerns that people have about information. Although people may be mildly irked by not knowing the latest news, they show far greater concern about other experiences that involve their *personal* information. We are sure that you personally have endured each of the following disturbing experiences with your own information:

Lost personal data: This is the deeply worrying experience of being unable to locate important information that you *know* you have, whether in the form of a lost document, contact name, or number, or an email that contains important information. This experience can be especially galling if you have made careful attempts to organize this information in order to avoid exactly this problem.

Large, disorganized personal collections of unclear value: The ease of capturing and sharing information means that we all have large collections of personal data, including photos, music, messages, documents, and even emails. We make strenuous efforts to collect such information and would be mortified to lose it if our hard disks crashed or our PCs or phones were stolen. However, for many of us, our actual experiences with these collections are very disappointing for two contradictory but related reasons: On the one hand, it's hard to reliably access valuable information from within our collections. On the other hand, browsing our collections draws attention to the fact we are acquiring large amounts of information that seems to be of low value.

Failing to deal with time-sensitive information that requires action: Another common, depressing experience concerns time-sensitive personal information that requires you to act in some way. This is particularly pernicious in email, in which we often overlook time-sensitive requests for information or deadlines for action. Again, an infuriating aspect of this experience is that we have often taken great care to create reminders or to organize information so as to guarantee that these deadlines are registered and met.

This is an incomplete list, but these negative experiences share an important unifying theme that makes them different from prevailing theoretical accounts that focus on acquiring novel public information: None of the preceding experiences concern *new* information. In each case, the problem concerns a failure to organize or structure information so as to facilitate its *reuse*. All the examples involve information that is *personal*, concerning our own collections rather than vast public databases. Far from the problems of explorers seeking out new informative worlds, these problems instead are closer to home. However, to address these problems we need to better understand how we curate our personal information, and for this we need new theories and approaches.

The first aim of this book is to argue that we need to reconceptualize our view of information and what we do with it. We need to move beyond the prevailing *consumer* characterization, which regards information as a public resource containing novel data that people seek out, consume, and then discard. Instead, this book will promote a different view of people's informational concerns. Much of the time, people are manipulating *familiar* information, using it as a personal resource that they keep, manage, and (sometimes repeatedly) exploit. We call this alternate view *information curation*.

If we accept this alternate view, then we need to better understand what curation involves. This book will argue that information curation is characterized by different processes than those in classic information science theory. A critical aspect of curation is that the person who *organizes* the information is also the person who *retrieves* it. This makes curation a different sort of game from consumption, one that follows different sets of rules than other information science fields.

Curation as Self-Directed Communication

One way to conceptualize curation is in terms of a communication metaphor. Other information science fields view the goal of information management as designing a communication channel between two people who have very different roles: An *information professional* (e.g., a website designer or a librarian) organizes target information so that an *information consumer* at the receiving end of the communication channel can locate and use that information. However, because information consumers differ from each other in their profession, education, sociocultural background, and intended use of information, the information professional is generally restricted to exploiting only user-independent attributes when organizing information. This is a one-size-fits-all approach in which every user sees information organized in the same way.

Curating personal information, on the other hand, is different because the person who stores the information and decides on its organization is the same person who later retrieves it (see figure 1.1). Curation therefore can be seen as a special kind of communication: a solipsistic interaction between a person and him- or herself at two different times: the time of storage and the

Figure 1.1
The person who stores the information and decides on its organization is the same person who later retrieves it.

time of retrieval. This alternative perspective led the authors to develop a technical approach to designing new technologies for curation. We call this approach *user subjective* because it relies on the fact that the ways in which people construe and organize their own information are personal.

The user-subjective approach takes advantage of this unique feature, arguing that when organizing personal collections, curation systems should make systematic use of *subjective, user-dependent* attributes. Curation systems should capture these subjective attributes when a user interacts with each information item (either automatically or by using direct manipulation[1] design) in order to help the user later retrieve that item. The user-subjective design approach is described in detail in part III.

The self-directed nature of curation also transforms the access process. In classic information management, retrieval explores novel public data, for which success often means finding information that satisfies certain general properties (e.g., "cheap flights to Spain") and multiple items may satisfy each query. In PIM, information access involves familiar, personally organized information. This leads to a further critical difference concerning retrieval of public versus personal information. When accessing personal information, a user often has a *specific item* in mind—making the criterion for success much more stringent. Of course, such prior knowledge often makes retrieval easier. During access, users may recognize the target item quickly. As a result, they do not have to scrutinize the item to determine its relevance as they would a novel web page. In other ways, accessing personal information is more difficult. When the target is specific information, retrieval becomes harder: It is successful only if that particular item is found, and there may be strong feelings of frustration following a failure to locate the item (Whittaker, Bergman, and Clough 2010).

The Emergence of Large Personal Data Collections

A critical motivation for an improved understanding of curation is that each of us now has large, complex accumulations of valued personal information that demand organization. Consumption models are focused on new information, arguing that we are continually seeking out novel public resources rather than acting with the information that we already have. If these models are correct, then we should not expect people to preserve personal archives for future consumption. One strong argument for the incompleteness of the consumption model is that people now keep huge amounts of personal information. A minute's reflection will reveal that people persistently engage in active and extensive preservation and curation behaviors, leading them to build large personal archives. Much as we might want to, we do not immediately delete each email we receive once we have read or replied to it. After successfully completing a document or presentation, we do not immediately transfer it to the trash. We preserve cherished photos and personal emails over periods of years.

There are many examples of people compiling, preserving, and managing personal collections for future exploitation. Let's examine some simple statistics about the huge amounts of information that people keep in such collections. These statistics offer a sense of the scale of the curation problem that we all experience.

Email is an obvious place to start. Whittaker, Bellotti, and Gwizdka (2007) summarize eight studies of email use, showing that people archive a huge number of messages, with an average of around 2,846 messages kept, although researchers may retain much larger archives (Fisher et al. 2006). A more recent study that monitored daily email usage over several months for 345 users showed that the average email archive consists of 2,568 messages (Whittaker et al. 2011). People also keep a large number of personal files, such as documents, spreadsheets, and presentations. Boardman and Sasse (2004) found an average of around 2,200 personal files stored on people's hard drives, and a recent study of digital photos found an average of over 4,000 personal pictures (Whittaker, Bergman, and Clough 2010), although the exponential growth of digital photography means that this number is certain to be an underestimate of current personal photo archives. Studies of web bookmarking show that people also preserve hundreds of bookmarks (Abrams, Baecker, and Chignell 1998; Aula, Jhaveri, and Kaki 2005; Boardman and Sasse 2004; Catledge and Pitkow 1995; Cockburn and Greenberg

2000). Of course, these behaviors are not limited to the digital domain: Whittaker and Hirschberg (2001) looked at paper archives and found that even after the emergence of the Internet, people still amassed huge amounts of personal paper data. That study found that on average researchers stored sixty-two kilograms of paper, equivalent to a pile of phone directories thirty meters high.

People do not only passively keep this information; they also make strenuous attempts to actively curate it to promote future exploitation. Bellotti et al. (2005) found that people spend 10 percent of their overall time in email filing and organizing their messages, leading to an average of 244 folders in their email collections—although a more recent study logging daily folder counts over several months suggests a smaller average of 46.89 folders (Whittaker et al. 2011). Personal computer files also show high levels of active organization, with people averaging fifty-seven folders and an average depth of 3.3 subfolders (Boardman and Sasse 2004). Studies of web bookmarking also show active organizational efforts, leading to an average of seventeen folders with complex subfolder structures (Abrams, Baecker, and Chignell 1998; Aula, Jhaveri, and Kaki 2005). Marshall (2008a, 2008b) describes the arcane organizations that result from attempts to curate information over many years.

Although it is obvious that consumption is important for some types of rapidly changing transient public information (e.g., news, entertainment), curation is a critical process. Furthermore, curation seems destined to become even more important. New technologies—such as ubiquitous sensors, medical or fitness trackers, digital video, and wearable cameras like Google Glass—make it increasingly easy to capture new types of personal data. This trend, along with continued increases in cheap digital storage, means that people's hard drives are filling up with huge collections of personal photos, videos, and music (Bell and Gemmell 2009; Kalnikaité et al. 2010; Marshall 2008a, 2008b; Sellen and Whittaker 2010; Whittaker et al. 2012).

One obvious objection to the importance of curation is that we spend large amounts of time accessing public resources such as the web. However, new research shows that even in this arena we often are not seeking novel information. Accessing the web usually entails reaccessing previously visited resources. Various studies have shown that most web behavior concerns reaccess. In other words, people revisit information they have already viewed. Between 58 percent and 81 percent of all user accesses are of pages that the user has accessed previously (Cockburn and Greenberg 2000; Obendorf et al. 2007; Tauscher and Greenberg 1997). Again, this suggests a pattern of curation and reuse rather than one-time consumption.

If these arguments are correct, we need to rethink our theories of how we interact with information. Prior systems and models of information emphasize consumption of public data (Belkin 1980; Ellis and Haugan 1997; Kuhlthau 1991; Marchionini 1997; Wilson 1981, 1994; Pirolli 2007; Pirolli and Card 1995). Indeed, until recently, limits on archival storage made it impossible to create and keep significant personal digital archives. The growth of personal archives and their exploitation, however, suggests a need to develop theories of curation. These new theories must explain the processes underlying active preservation and organization of personal information for future retrieval and exploitation. We need to look beyond models of information foraging and information seeking and think about practices for preserving and curating information. Agricultural practices allowed our ancestors to cultivate food resources for future needs, thus freeing themselves from the vagaries of foraging in an unpredict-able environment. In the same way, we need new theories, tools, and practices for curation to help support these pervasive, future-oriented information exploitation activities.

Defining Personal Information

What exactly do we mean by *personal information*? Our informal description of personal collections included a wide range of information types originating from a variety of different sources. One critical point to note here is that not all personal data is self-created. In addition to personally created documents and photos, personal archives also contain emails, texts, and social media created and shared by others. Personal collections can also contain data that were originally accessed from public archives, such as maps, or links to useful online resources. This public data might be bookmarked or saved to a local disk to increase its availability. What unifies all these disparate data types into a personal collection is their projected future value for a user. Users seek to preserve and organize personal data them-selves because they want to ensure access to that data at some future time. What defines personal information therefore is not the type or provenance of information, but rather that users stra-tegically choose to organize the information themselves with an eye to its future access. In other words, personal information is information that users actively curate.

What is involved in curation? Next, we present the *curation life cycle* and describe the processes by which we keep, manage, and exploit personal information. We elaborate on the relation-ships among these three processes and on the challenges involved in each. Then, we discuss important distinctions between different types of personal information that have direct implications for curation, such as whether information is unique and whether it requires action.

The Curation Life Cycle

Curation involves *future-oriented* activities—that is, a set of practices that selects and manages personal information in ways that are intended to promote future exploitation of that information (see figure 1.2). We begin this section by introducing a simple, three-stage model of the curation life cycle that involves keeping, managing, and exploiting personal data. This model is based on the highly influential PIM framework proposed by Jones (Jones 2007b; Jones and Teevan 2007). Our three-stage model also shares important overlaps with the analysis presented by

Figure 1.2
Use curation techniques to avoid this sort of office problem.

Marshall (2008a, 2008b). Although curation has been discussed in the context of public information (Kuny 1997; Lesk 1998; Rothenberg 1995), the underlying processes are radically different when organizing personal data, as you have seen. While discussing the framework, we provide examples from our own studies.

Keeping

We encounter new information all the time. Much of this encountered information is completely irrelevant to us. Other ephemeral pieces of information, such as news or trivia, may be of little future utility once we have registered them. When we eliminate these straightforward cases, the decision about what information to keep in our personal collections becomes more complex. This decision is difficult because we have to predict the information needs of our future selves. We know that we will need *some* of this newly encountered information in the future, but how do we decide exactly what is worth keeping? What principles govern decisions about the sorts of information we keep (Jones 2004, 2007a, 2007b; Whittaker and Hirschberg 2001)? There are obvious costs to keeping information, so how do we decide which information will have significant future value? What makes that information worth those costs (Jones, Bruce et al. 2005; Marshall 2008a, 2008b)? Keeping is a complex decision process influenced by many factors, including the type of information being evaluated, when we expect we will need it, and the context in which we imagine that it will be needed. There are obvious benefits for keeping information that we believe will be useful, but if we keep too much, then we incur both organizational costs and increased retrieval difficulty resulting from having to access a larger archive. There are also strategic trade-offs for keeping information ourselves, rather than relying on regenerating that same information from public resources, or obtaining it from collaborators (Bergman, Whittaker, and Falk 2014; Whittaker and Hirschberg 2001).

Information items—whether they are documents, email messages, photos, or web pages—have differing future utility and consequently will be evaluated in different ways. Transient information encountered on a public web page will be judged differently than a personal document crafted over several days or an email sent by an important colleague. The technologies that we use to generate and encounter information also have an effect on how likely we are to keep information. Take the example of photography: Digital technology now has made it easy to take many photos, and preserving digital photos is inexpensive because storage technology is now so cheap. One consequence of this situation is that people are keeping many more photos than in the past, when taking photos was expensive, developing them was laborious, and careful physical organization and storage were essential (Sarvas and Frohlich 2011). However, the ease of capturing photos may have important downstream consequences for retrieval, and we need to take these consequences into account when deciding what to keep. Keeping large numbers of near-duplicate or low-quality photos may make it harder to find genuinely valuable photos that we want to access again (Whittaker, Bergman, and Clough 2010).

Management

We now turn to issues related to how people manage the information they have decided to keep. Having chosen to preserve certain information, how should we manage that information in ways that will guarantee future value? Recall that curation is like a communication that we have with our future selves, in which the goal is to organize information to improve the likelihood that we will find it again. Like the keeping decision process, communicating with our future selves is a difficult process that may not always succeed. It may involve actively organizing information in certain ways to provide future retrieval cues that will enable us to reconstruct where information is located. For example, carefully chosen folder and file names can trigger successful retrieval as we navigate our file systems, or we might place important files on our computer desktops if it is critical that we are reminded about them.

A key factor people have to take into account is the trade-off between the effort they invest in managing information and the projected payoff during exploitation. Different ways of managing information have different costs and payoffs. As information curators, we have to decide between intensive versus less demanding organizational methods. Intensive methods are more likely to engender higher information yields, but at the cost of greater up-front management efforts. Investing time in these intensive methods must be evaluated against using less demanding methods that offer less predictable returns. For example, we might apply systematic organization to our files by filing information into structured folders. This information should then be easier to access—providing that the structure matches the context in which we wish to retrieve the information. However, this filing strategy imposes a heavy burden on the information curator because each new piece of information must be analyzed and structured in a particular way. Alternatively, we may adopt a more relaxed approach and allow physical information to accumulate in loosely organized piles on our desks or let email messages pile up in our inbox. This laissez-faire tactic reduces the up-front costs of organizing information but may make it harder to locate critical information when we need it (Malone 1983; Whittaker 2005; Whittaker and Hirschberg 2001; Whittaker and Sidner 1996).

Management is complex, because it requires users to predict when or how information will be accessed. To create effective organizations, users have to anticipate the context in which they will be accessing information. As a result, they may not always be successful in organizing information in ways that facilitate future retrieval. People spend time constructing systematic organizations for web and email data, although such organizations do not always improve retrieval (Aula, Jhaveri, and Kaki 2005; Whittaker et al. 2011). The opposite is also true. People fail to organize personal photos with the result that they are unable to retrieve these in the long-term (Whittaker, Bergman, and Clough 2010).

The management process is also iterative, and we modify our personal information systems in an adaptive way. We repeatedly revisit and restructure information related to ongoing tasks to meet our current needs. People also remember better the organization of recently or frequently visited information—making such information more straightforward to access. In contrast, other types of information may be infrequently accessed, such as photos that are stored for the long term. Infrequent access may mean that users are less familiar with how such information is organized. They may also fail to discover that their photo collections need to be systematically restructured to support effective access (Whittaker, Bergman, and Clough 2010).

Management also may have repetitive properties. Some people habitually cull information that has turned out to be of little value and that is compromising the uptake of clearly valuable information. People occasionally spring-clean their email inboxes, deleting old or irrelevant information (Whittaker and Sidner 1996). However, it is abundantly clear that people find such cleanup activities difficult, not only because cleanup requires judgments about the projected value of information, but also because there may be emotional commitment to keeping information that one has invested time and effort in organizing (Jones 2007a, 2007b; Marshall 2008a, 2008b; Whittaker and Hirschberg 2001).

Finally, new cloud technologies promise to change management in critical ways. Technologies such as Google Drive, Dropbox, and Microsoft OneDrive allow multiple users to co-organize shared repositories. This field is known as *group information management* or GIM (Erickson 2006). GIM offers potential management efficiencies because users can exploit organizations created by others, rather than each person independently managing his or her personal information. A potential downside of GIM is that groups may fail to agree on how shared information should be organized to optimize retrieval (Berlin et al. 1993; Rader 2009). We include discussion of GIM in this book because, as in PIM, GIM requires a collaborating group to actively organize its information. In addition, when a group of people start collaborating, it typically faces a dilemma related to how to share the files the group creates together: Should the group distribute the files as email attachments and then store them in personal repositories (relying on PIM techniques) or store shared files in a common repository (relying on GIM techniques)? Problems arise in GIM when the person who organizes information is not the person who retrieves it.

Exploitation

Exploitation refers to the process of retrieving information. Exploitation is at the heart of curation practices. If we cannot successfully exploit the personal information we preserve, then keeping decisions and management activity will have been futile. What are effective ways to access curated information? Following our communication metaphor, if retrieval is to be successful we have to understand what our past selves were trying to tell us. Successful exploitation clearly relates to keeping and management practices. Careful attempts to organize valuable personal information should make it easier to reaccess that data. However, new technology potentially reduces the need to actively organize. Emerging technologies such as desktop search (Cutrell, Dumais, and Teevan 2006; Dumais et al. 2003; Russell and Lawrence 2007) or GIM (Bergman, Whittaker, and Falk 2014; Berlin et al. 1993; Massey, Lennig, and Whittaker 2014) promise to reduce the overhead of organizing our files because these technologies no longer require us to organize or navigate to files manually ourselves.

A user's goal when attempting to retrieve an information item is to put that information to use. On successful exploitation, users might therefore go on to modify a retrieved document, respond to emails they have relocated to the inbox, or integrate web page information into documents they are writing. Although important, these follow-on activities will not be discussed in this book. Our discussion of exploitation will be limited to the action of attempting to retrieve an information item. We retrieve personal information in two main ways:

One straightforward way to access information is to manually navigate to it (Bergman et al. 2008). For information items such as files, we navigate within self-generated hierarchies of folders and subfolders. People usually traverse their organizational hierarchies manually (Bergman et al. 2008; Fitchett and Cockburn 2015; Teevan et al. 2004). They visually and recursively scan within each folder (either actively by sorting the items by attribute or by using the system default) until they locate the folder that contains the target item.

Search is another way to access personal information. In this method, desktop search is an important technology that allows users to locate information within their own file systems by using keyword queries, in the same way they conduct web searches (Cutrell, Dumais, and Teevan 2006; Russell and Lawrence 2007). Search involves two steps: query generation and result selection. First, a user generates a query by specifying one or more of the following properties of the target item: at least one word related to the name of the information item; some of the text that the item contains (full text search); any metadata attribute relating to the item (e.g., the date it was created). The desktop search engine then returns a set of results, from which the user selects the relevant item. Note that even if people rely on search rather than manual navigation to refind personal information, they still have to generate relevant search terms to guarantee success; this requires them to mentally reconstruct important aspects of the target document (e.g., title, keywords, date).

There are advantages and disadvantages to both methods. Navigation, being incremental, offers the user visual feedback and control at each access stage (Barreau and Nardi 1995; Bergman et al. 2008). However, in the case of deeply nested folder hierarchies, navigation can be laborious because of the multiple levels users have to traverse. Search is potentially more flexible and efficient, allowing users to specify multiple properties of the target file (Lansdale 1988). However, search is reliant on being able to remember distinctive properties of the target item in order to generate appropriate search terms. We will compare these two methods at length in chapters 5 and 8.

There is also a third approach, which analyses prior user actions. It capitalizes on the fact that many information items are repeatedly accessed in PIM and gives the user a direct way to retrieve recently accessed items. For files, lists of recent documents are available, either at the OS level or within an application. A large portion of file retrievals involve using such recent documents lists (Fitchett and Cockburn 2015). On the web, there is also strong evidence for reliance on recency (Dumais et al. 2003; Obendorf et al. 2007; Cockburn and Greenberg 2000). Browser technology also supports recency: Users can access recently viewed web pages via features such as the back button, web history, and autocompletion (exploiting past user searches). A related method is frequency based, such that browsers such as Chrome and Safari display icons of the web pages most frequently accessed by the current user. However, recency-based methods depend on successful previous retrieval and therefore must be combined with one of the other methods (Fitchett and Cockburn 2015). Therefore, this book will not focus heavily on recency approaches.

Interrelations between Keeping, Management, and Exploitation

It is obvious that there are close relations between keeping, management, and exploitation processes in the curation life cycle. For example, successful exploitation is highly dependent on the information people choose to keep as well as the methods they use to manage it. Keeping information does not necessarily guarantee that it will be successfully exploited. The more information we keep, the more effort has to go into organizing and maintaining it. Critically, having more information may increase the difficulty of exploitation; finding what one needs may be harder when there is more kept information, and irrelevant information can distract.

Past outcomes may also influence future curation behaviors. Exploitation success may influence future keeping and management practices. If certain information is difficult to re-access, people may conclude that there is little point in keeping it in future. In the same way, exploitation failures may cause people to change their management methods. If users realize that certain types of organization are less successful in promoting access, they may change those methods.

Chapters 2, 3, and 4 describe the different processes involved in curation in detail—namely, keeping, management, and exploitation. However, before we tackle these topics, it is important to discuss fundamental differences in the properties of different types of information.

Information Properties

Not all information items are equivalent. We need to distinguish between different properties of information items, as these differences have implications for how that item will be curated.

Informative vs. Actionable Items

Compare, for example, a typical email message and a page found in a web search. One crucial property of many email messages is that they require the recipient to *do something*, whether to respond to a question, arrange a meeting, or provide some information. Such email messages are *actionable*, because the message recipient is expected to respond in some way, often within a specific timeframe ("let me know about this before Tuesday"). In contrast, information items found during a web search are potentially informative—but do not usually require users to act. A web page may be engaging, but there is usually no requirement to process the information on the page to meet a given deadline. Of course, this *information* versus *action* distinction does not map neatly to computer applications. Not every message in email is actionable (e.g., when people send us FYIs) and not every web page is purely informative (e.g., when a page contains a request to complete a form).

This distinction between information and action has critical implications for how we treat personal information. For reasons that will become clear, it is often impossible to discharge actionable items immediately. Their time-sensitive nature therefore means that they have to be managed in a specific way. People have to implement strategies to remind themselves about their commitments with respect to the undischarged action item. These reminding strategies might involve creating to-do email folders or leaving active documents on the desktop. Failure to implement such strategies can have severe implications for job success and productivity: we cannot forget to respond to important requests from our bosses, even when we are inundated with other commitments. In contrast, the manner in which we deal with informative items usually is more discretionary. Such items usually do not need to be actively processed to meet deadlines, so it is less critical that we enact dedicated reminding strategies to ensure that they are dealt with appropriately.

Information Uniqueness

Another critical information property is *uniqueness*, which has strong implications for how we deal with personal information. Certain types of information (such as personal files that we create ourselves) may reside only on our computers. As a result, an individual may be the only person in the world who has access to certain items. Those who have lost data following a system crash are only too aware that if they do not take personal responsibility for backing up unique data, then that data will not be preserved for future access (Marshall 2008a, 2008b). In contrast, other data in our personal collections is not unique—giving us more chance of recovering it. Public information—such as web data—may reside on multiple servers and may be recoverable even if we cannot relocate our personal copies. Other data lie somewhere in between. Someone may be able to ask coworkers to regenerate a copy of an important email message that he or she has temporarily mislaid or erroneously deleted, but there is no guarantee that coworkers will have kept that information.

It is important to note that uniqueness is defined personally—relative to our own goals and interests. Innumerable unique information items exist in the world, but as curators we are concerned only about taking decisive action to preserve those items relevant to ourselves. Other people's information may be equally important to them, but there is no reason we should be concerned to preserve it, unless of course we work with those other people. This personal uniqueness is often associated with information that we have invested effort in creating. If we have dedicated substantial time to generating an information item (e.g., an extended personal document, a carefully crafted presentation, or a collection of wedding photos), then that information will be something that we make enormous efforts to preserve, in part because of the effort involved in regenerating it.

Uniqueness has a huge impact on our management strategies. No one else will take care of our unique personal data. We personally need to create reliable structures for reaccessing highly important personal data, such as passwords, tax forms, passport details, or financial records, even when we rarely need to access this information. Personally created documents also tend to be unique and need to be carefully organized. This is also somewhat true for email messages; we need to have reliable methods for reaccessing emails because we cannot always rely on others to keep the important messages that we need. In contrast, web pages are different. They are generally more easily recoverable (via search or browsing) even if we have not bookmarked them. In addition, because we have not usually been responsible for generating their content, we are not as concerned if we cannot recover the information they contain.

Table 1.1 lists the key properties of common classes of information, such as paper, electronic files, email, photos, and web documents. These classes are different with respect to both action orientation and uniqueness. Personal documents and email messages are often actionable. Documents and personal photos tend to be unique. These differences have strong implications for curation. The uniqueness of personal documents and personal photos leads people to be very conservative and to keep most of these items. People also have to preserve actionable items such as email messages and personal documents in ways that promote appropriate, timely action.

Table 1.1
Primary properties of different types of information involved in curation

Information type	Actionable or informative?	Uniqueness	Active/passive accumulation
Personal paper and electronic documents	Actionable if self-created and current; long-term archives tend to be informative	Unique if self-created or annotated	Passive
Email	Often actionable; long-term archives tend to be informative	Ranges from unique to nonunique mass mailings	Passive
Contacts	Actionable	Nonunique	Active (phone) and passive (email)
Personal photos	Neither actionable nor informative: affective	Predominantly unique	Passive
Web	Informative	Nonunique	Active

Accumulation and Prominence: Active vs. Passive Archiving

A final important information property concerns whether information accumulates automatically or whether a user action has to be taken to preserve it. Consider the differences between emails and web browsing. Users don't have to decide to keep their emails; emails accumulate by default, unless a user takes action to delete them. In contrast, the pages that are accessed during a web search are registered in the user's search history but have very low prominence as part of a user's personal archive unless an action is taken, such as actively bookmarking them.

This distinction has important implications for keeping, which is a critical decision process for web documents. Users have to evaluate whether each page they encounter is important enough to actively include in their personal archives—enough so, for example, to bookmark it. In contrast, other media (such as email) accumulate automatically into one's personal archive. In the case of email, keeping decisions involve determining whether to delete information that is already in the archive by expunging it from the archive.

PIM Behaviors and Technology Change

At this point, a thought may have occurred to you: The goal of this book is to study people's interactions with their personal information, but isn't scientific study made difficult by the fact that new PIM technologies are introduced on a regular basis? For example, hasn't digital photography been transformed by new devices allowing us to capture and organize massive numbers of photos? Aren't social media, smartphones, and wearable devices creating vast new archives of personal data of radically different kinds that will require new theories and methods for PIM?

This is an important objection. However, one key theme of this book is that fundamental PIM problems are surprisingly resistant to technology change. Part I reviews studies of paper, email, and web documents. In some cases, these studies were conducted almost twenty years ago, but the problems that emerge are depressingly familiar, even though the technologies are different. Despite apparent technology improvements, we still forget to deal with vital actionable items, find it hard to judge the value of new information, keep large amounts of information of questionable value, and fail to retrieve important information that we have made stringent efforts to organize. As you will see, these problems generalize across different media: Many of the overkeeping problems that we encounter with our email also arise with photos and files. Users struggle to decide how to organize information to guarantee future access, whether working with files, photos, documents, or web pages. This fact suggests that PIM problems are deep-rooted and general, rather than dependent on a specific technology or type of data. As a simple illustration, Google's flagship email product, Inbox by Gmail, released in 2015, seeks to address the problem of remembering actionable emails—a problem that was first identified almost twenty years before (Whittaker and Sidner 1996).

We return to this point in part II, in which we evaluate exciting new technologies like search, tagging, and GIM. These technologies have been proposed as potential solutions to PIM problems, both reducing the need to actively manage information and also providing new, efficient ways to access our personal data. Again, the results of empirical evaluations are somewhat surprising; despite intuitive advantages of emerging technologies, it seems that unfashionable folders are still preferred. This brings us to the third important scientific contribution of this book, which is to provide theoretical cognitive explanations for the continued importance of folders and hierarchical navigation. Part III describes our own approach, incorporating our prior findings to offer a set of new principles for PIM technologies that address these general problems. We return to new technologies in Conclusions and Future Directions, where we analyze which emerging technologies may affect PIM.

Summary

This chapter argued that curation is a critical information management problem. We first contrasted curation, in which users are responsible for organizing their own personal information, with traditional information management models that focus on consumption of public information that has been organized by others. We further detailed the need to better understand curation by characterizing the extent and complexity of personal archives. We introduced the key curation life cycle processes of keeping, management, and exploitation, and described the interrelations between them, and presented a taxonomy of different information types, describing different properties of uniqueness, action/information orientation, and accumulation. Finally, we explored the relationship between underlying PIM processes and technology, arguing that PIM processes are deep-rooted and somewhat resistant to technology change.

In the remainder of part I, we will discuss each of these life cycle processes in detail, describing how people keep, manage, and exploit their personal information, and will analyze the impact of these different information types on curation processes. As we noted earlier, we will focus on our own research rather than reviewing the entire PIM literature.

2 Keeping

Overview, Problems, and Strategies

Keeping concerns the fundamental decision of whether to retain or delete the information that we encounter. We cannot keep every piece of information we are exposed to, because of various costs:

• *Management costs*: We need to organize information if we are to obtain value from it. The more we keep, the more management effort is required. Some visions of new technology suggest that in the future our information will be organized automatically, but these technologies are not yet in place. Indeed, in part II, we explore whether these technologies will *ever* effectively replace the need for manual organization.

• *Exploitation costs*: Keeping information of low value increases the difficulty of retrieval. Keeping too many items can be distracting and inefficient if manual navigation is used for access. To address this, there are those who contend that future retrieval will be entirely *search based*, reducing exploitation costs regardless of how much we keep. Chapter 5 reviews extensive evidence that challenges this view, suggesting instead that navigation is users' preferred access strategy regardless of search engine quality. Chapter 8 explains the preference for navigation.

Keeping decisions are a fact of life. Every day we receive new email messages, create new files and folders, and browse new websites. Some of this new information is of little long-term value, but other information is task-critical or needs to be preserved for the long term. Data from Boardman and Sasse (2004) suggest that users acquire an average of five new files per day, and one bookmark every five days. Other studies indicate that people acquire one new contact per day (Whittaker, Jones, and Terveen 2002) and around five digital photos (Whittaker, Bergman, and Clough 2010). Numbers of emails acquired per day are more variable across studies, ranging between five and sixty (Whittaker, Bellotti, and Gwizdka 2007), with the most reliable estimates suggesting that twenty-four messages are acquired each day (Whittaker et al. 2011). However, these statistics are an oversimplification of the complexity of keeping decisions. The statistics record *positive* keeping decisions but fail to register the many decisions to discard information judged to be of little value. To be more specific, statistics suggest that users receive an average of forty-four email messages per day; focusing exclusively on the twenty-four messages that users decide to keep overlooks the twenty decisions to delete or ignore irrelevant information. For email alone, making the highly conservative assumption that email volumes will not change over our lifetimes, this equates to over 350,000 keeping decisions over a fifty-year digital life.

We know from various interview and survey studies that people find it difficult to decide what information they want to keep (Bergman et al. 2009; Boardman and Sasse 2004; Jones 2004, 2007a, 2007b; Whittaker and Hirschberg 2001; Whittaker and

Sidner 1996). Why are keeping decisions so difficult? One reason is that they require us to *predict the future*. To decide what to keep, we have to determine the probable future value of an information item (Bruce 2005).

This is a general psychological problem. A great deal of psychological research shows that people are bad at making many types of decisions that involve their future. Such prediction requires people to reason about hypothetical situations, a task at which people are notoriously poor. People's predictions are also subject to various types of bias. For example, they expect the future to be very much like the present, and their predictions are unduly influenced by recent or easily recalled events (Gilbert 2009; Kahneman and Tversky 1979). People are also loss averse, so thinking about information in a context in which it might be deleted leads them to overvalue it (Kahneman and Tversky 1979; Whittaker and Hirschberg 2001).

We now will review various studies that examine people's keeping decisions for paper archives, email messages, contacts, web pages, and personal photos. Somewhat curiously, in spite of the prevalence of keeping decisions, relatively little research has looked at keeping directly. By focusing on what information people keep, these studies also inform us about general properties of personal archives by identifying what information people think is valuable to archive and why.

Before turning to these studies, we must first clarify our focus. The main goal of this book is to study curation processes for personal *digital* information. Why then are we describing how people keep and manage *paper*? The explanation is that people treat personal paper archives in ways that are very similar to how they treat personal digital information. In other words, studies of paper curation reveal general principles that also apply to digital contexts. We will see strong commonalities across paper and digital media. In both settings, people keep a mixture of personally created and publicly available documents. They also find it hard to predict the future value of information in both settings and therefore overkeep, resulting in large personal collections that contain items of unclear value.

Keeping Paper

One of the few studies of keeping examines work-related paper archives (Whittaker and Hirschberg 2001). One methodological problem with investigating keeping lies in finding contexts in which people are explicitly focused on the keeping decision. Our study identified one such situation: Participants had to relocate to smaller offices. Their new offices had reduced personal storage space compared with their existing offices, although extra storage was provided in public locations. Reduced storage space meant people had to decide which information to keep and what to throw away. When we interviewed our participants, they had all recently sorted through their personal paper archives in preparation for the move. The reduction in local storage motivated careful reflection as well as sorting and discarding of existing data. In interviewing and surveying workers during the move, we capitalized on the fact that they had very recently handled most of their paper data, forcing them to identify criteria for determining what to keep and what to discard. We took a *multimethod* approach, collecting both qualitative and quantitative keeping data. We strongly believe in this multimethod research approach; you will find it represented in various chapters of this book.

Discarding Behavior

Participants experienced major problems in deciding what to keep and what to throw away. As the psychology literature on loss aversion (Kahneman and Tversky 1979) would suggest, there was a bias toward retention. Even after spending large amounts of time deciding what to discard, participants still retained huge archives. In preparation for their move, people spent almost nine hours rationalizing their data and reported that this was a difficult process. In spite of these efforts, the amount of information that people actually threw away was small compared with what they kept. They discarded just 22 percent of their original archives, with the final preserved archive occupying on average more than eighteen mover's boxes.

We looked at the characteristics of not only what people kept but also what was discarded. As expected, a subset of the discarded data was once-valuable information that had become obsolete. As jobs, personal interests, or company strategies change, the value of some information decreases. However, not all discarded information underwent the transition from valuable to obsolete. For example, 23 percent of discarded data were *unread*. Why would people retain information they have never even looked at? Two general problems contributed to this accumulation of superfluous information. First, people experience problems with information overload, leading them to only partially process incoming information. Second, they engage in deferred evaluation of what to keep—causing them to acquire large amounts of data that later turn out to be extraneous. Furthermore, information overload and deferred evaluation are not unique to paper archives: We will see the same processes at work for email and digital files, contacts, and photos.

Information overload occurs when people have insufficient time to process all the information to which they are exposed. One consequence of information overload is that nonurgent information is never processed. Nonurgent data are set aside, often in optimistically named "to read" piles, and accumulate indefinitely; the same time pressures that prevent complete processing of incoming data also prevent rationalizing (cleanup) of archives. Consequently, people seldom discover that their unread, nonurgent documents are superfluous until exceptional circumstances—such as an office move or purchasing a new computer—force them to scrutinize their archives.

Yet even when people do find the time to examine new information systematically, uncertainty of the future value of that information means they are often highly conservative—postponing final judgments about utility until some unspecified future date. Some people deliberately *defer evaluation* of incoming information, allowing time to pass so as to make better-informed judgments about information utility. Often, these post hoc judgments are based on whether information actually was ever used.

Deferred evaluation means that people retain information of unclear value just in case it later turns out to be useful. Judgments about potential future utility are made more difficult because the value of data can change over time. Knowing that the value of information can change also leads some people to postpone the keeping decision so long as there is still archival space.

Accumulating unprocessed data and deferring evaluation are good from the conservative perspective in that potentially valuable information is not lost. However, the problem with this approach is that people seldom revisit their archives to rationalize them, so archives end up containing considerable amounts of information of dubious value. Thus, 74 percent of the participants in our paper study had not cleaned out their archives for over a year. Furthermore, very few cleanups occurred spontaneously: 84 percent arose from extrinsic events such as job changes or office moves. This infrequency of cleanups means that many items often are not discovered to be superfluous until they have been stored for some time.

To sum up, this study illustrates important aspects of keeping. First, there is a strong bias toward retaining information. When extraordinary events such an office move occur, people discard only 22 percent of their data. The study also shows key reasons for such overkeeping. Information overload and deferred evaluation mean that incoming information is incompletely processed, leading personal archives to be polluted by marginally relevant data. Rather than discarding once-valuable information that is now of little utility, much of what people later discard is unprocessed information they have never properly evaluated, but kept "just in case."

What Do We Keep and Why Do We Keep It?

The same study also looked at the properties of the information people kept and their reasons for keeping it. One conjecture was that a large proportion of the information kept would be unique to that person. In contrast, we expected people to be much less likely to keep publicly available data. Why take responsibility for information that is available elsewhere?

Uniqueness clearly was important in determining whether users would preserve certain documents. Unique data are usually highly associated with their archiver. Three types of unique data accounted for 49 percent of people's archives: working notes, archives of completed projects, and legal documents, such as contracts or tax documents.

However, contrary to our expectations, uniqueness was not the sole criterion for deciding to keep data. To our surprise, only 49 percent of people's original archive was unique—with 36 percent consisting of copies of publicly available documents. We have already observed that personal collections contain a mix of self-created data and information accessed from public sources, such as the web—but we haven't addressed in detail *why* that is true. Why keep personal duplicates of readily available public documents, especially when doing so imposes additional workload to manage that information? Our paper study suggested four main reasons: availability, reminding, lack of trust in external stores, and sentiment.

Availability allows relevant materials to be at hand when people need them. Several people mentioned not wanting to experience the delay associated with refinding information or accessing it from the web. Other research shows that people are sometimes unable to refind public information they have successfully retrieved in the past (Wen 2003). In other words, people wanted to reduce their exploitation costs by keeping valued information close at hand in personal archives.

Reminding relates to availability and is critical for actionable information. Having a personal copy of a public document increases the likelihood that people will encounter that document, especially if the document is deliberately stored in a visible place. Personal copies are often created when an action has to be taken regarding a public document. A personal copy prompts people about outstanding actions associated with the document, or simply reminds them they are in possession of that information. Documents in public stores seem less capable of supporting reminding.

People also keep personal copies of public data because they *do not trust* other archival institutions to keep the documents they need. Distrust of external stores also extends to digital resources such as the web.

In addition to these functional reasons, people describe *sentimental* reasons for keeping information. People admit that certain information has little relevance for likely future activities, but they still can't part with it because it is part of their intellectual history or professional identity.

Another potential reason for keeping personal copies of publicly available documents is that they contain *personal annotations*. Other research has documented the utility of annotations while processing new information. Taking notes helps focus attention and improves comprehension of what is read or heard (Kalnikaité and Whittaker 2007, 2008a; Sellen and Harper 2002). Although most people make such annotations, they seem of little practical long-term use. Many people stated that annotations have transient value, becoming uninterpretable after some time has elapsed. This is consistent with recent studies of long-term note taking, which show that the utility of handwritten notes decreases rapidly even after a month (Kalnikaité and Whittaker 2007, 2008a). In other words, there may be less value to keeping annotated materials than people believe.

Keeping Email

We now turn to email and how we decide what messages we need to keep. Email is different from either self-created files or documents accessed on the web. One major difference is that a significant portion of the information we receive in email is *actionable*: We have to respond to it or process it, often within a specific time frame. This contrasts with most web-based information, which does not demand action. Another significant property of email is that most messages are generated by others, and in some cases these others are unfamiliar to us. This lack of familiarity sometimes makes it harder for people to evaluate the utility of such email information. A final different characteristic of email is its sheer variability. In our inboxes, we may see many different types of messages, including tasks or to-do items, documents or attachments, FYIs, appointments, social messages, and jokes (Whittaker and Sidner 1996). This heterogeneity makes the keeping decision rather different from the decision for other information types. In addition, although new email clients have emerged over the last twenty years, keeping challenges observed with older systems still remain problematic today. As a simple example, although current email systems make it possible to store every message we encounter, modern email clients such as Inbox by Gmail encourage users to make the keeping decision by "swiping" unimportant or discharged emails from view, allowing users to focus on more critical items.

Overall, we keep about 70 percent of our email messages (Dabbish et al. 2005), although numbers vary depending on the user population (Whittaker et al. 2011; Whittaker, Bellotti, and Gwizdka 2007). This seems a surprisingly high retention rate, given the apparent irrelevance of many of the email messages we receive, but it can be explained. We will discuss people's keeping behaviors for informative versus actionable messages separately, because keeping behavior is very different for each type.

Informative Messages

Informative messages make up about one-third (34 percent) of what is delivered in email (Dabbish et al. 2005). Informative messages are treated in a similar manner as paper documents.

As with paper archives, the keeping decision is often difficult: People find it hard to judge the value of incoming informative messages, so they use the deferral strategy. Rather than investing valuable time to definitively judge the value of a new informative message, users register its arrival but defer making a decision about it until they are more certain of its value. Deferred email messages are kept, potentially allowing more informed judgments to be made later.

Also as with paper archives, people experience information overload in email, which exacerbates the difficulty of deciding which information to keep. The sheer volume of incoming messages may lead people to defer completely reading each message until they have more time, and because they are constantly bombarded with more incoming messages, people often do not return to deferred messages (Whittaker and Sidner 1996). One factor contributing to whether an informative message is read is its length: Whittaker and Sidner found that the inbox contained a higher proportion of longer messages compared with the rest of people's email archives. This is consistent with the intuition that people leave longer messages in their inboxes for later reading.

Actionable Items

Actionable messages demand that we do something specific. In an ideal world (such as that inhabited by management consultants), we might process these messages just once, carrying out the required action and then deleting them. This is often referred to as the one-touch model. The advantages of the model are obvious: Touching a message just once means that people do not later forget to deal with it, and they do not have to reconstruct the context of old actionable messages repeatedly when they eventually process these. If messages are processed at once, it keeps the inbox clear for important incoming messages.

Some users try to adhere to this model; overall, users reply to 65 percent of actionable messages immediately (Dabbish et al. 2005). An immediate reply clearly reduces the chance that one will forget to act on a message. However, even when people do reply immediately, they still keep *85 percent* of actionable messages, suggesting that "one touch" does not accurately describe actual keeping practice.

Several factors may account for such retention. In some cases, one touch and an immediate reply are not possible. Many important email tasks are too complex or lengthy to be executed immediately (Bellotti et al. 2005; Venolia et al. 2001; Whittaker 2005; Whittaker and Sidner 1996), which leads to deferral of 37 percent of actionable messages (Dabbish et al. 2005). Another reason for deferral is that interdependent tasks arise that involve tight collaboration with others (Bellotti et al. 2005; Whittaker 2005). Interdependence results in both iteration and delays, because interdependent tasks often require multiple exchanges between collaborators (Bellotti et al. 2005; Venolia et al. 2001; Venolia and Neustaedter 2003; Whittaker and Sidner 1996). Collaborators may need to negotiate exactly what a collaborative email task involves or who will be responsible for each component of that task. One way to estimate the prevalence of interdependent email tasks is by determining how many messages form part of a conversational thread. Threading estimates range from 30 to 62 percent of messages

(Bellotti et al. 2003; Whittaker, Bellotti, and Gwizdka 2007), showing that interdependence is common.

The need to defer actionable messages has important consequences for keeping. Unless actions are discharged, messages are usually kept as reminders that they are still incomplete. Actionable messages therefore are almost always kept (only 0.5 percent are deleted). This figure is much higher than for informative messages, 30 percent of which are deleted. Furthermore, actionable messages have to be kept in a way that guarantees that they will be reencountered. It is no good deferring to-do email messages unless you have a method of guaranteeing that you will actually return to them. We revisit this issue in the next chapter, when we talk about email management strategies.

Keeping Contacts

Contact management is another area that demands careful keeping decisions. Whittaker, Jones, and Terveen (2002) explored the criteria people use for including someone in their contact lists. Our study mainly focused on contacts acquired through email, although we also looked at people's address books, rolodexes, calendars, and contact management programs. As we will see in chapter 10, keeping behaviors that relate to mobile phone contacts are somewhat different because of both constraints on screen size and the need to actively add contacts to one's address book.

We are overloaded again with respect to the contacts we encounter. We are copied on many messages, and we read web pages or posts from friends, colleagues, and strangers. Some of these people we want to interact with again; others may have been involved in one-off conversations that require no follow-up. Many email clients now automatically record contact emails and add them to the user's address book. However, many of these contacts are never revisited and even are unknown to the user. Contact management requires decisions both about the people for whom you will keep detailed information and about the types of information that you will keep about those people.

It is difficult to distinguish important future contacts among the many people that you are exposed to on a daily basis. As with paper and email archives, it is hard to intuit the future, to determine whether you will need to communicate with each person again. Whether someone is an important contact becomes clear only over time. Just as with email and paper deferral strategies, our study participants often *overkept* contact information, leading to huge rolodexes, overflowing booklets of business cards, and faded sticky notes scattered around their work areas. Even so, participants recorded detailed information about only a small portion of the contacts that they encountered.

Our investigation identified specific factors that were critical in determining important contacts. Just as with deferred evaluation in email and paper archives, the final keeping decision depends on past interaction with a contact, in particular the frequency and recency of communication. People also noted how difficult it was to make decisions about a contact's future value based on short-term interactions and scanty evidence. We saw the importance of long-term information in evaluating contacts: important contacts are those with whom we have repeated interactions over extended periods. As with email and paper, the decision to keep a specific contact is error-prone because of the difficulty of predicting long-term utility on the basis of brief initial interactions.

As part of the same study, we followed up with participants, presented them with contacts mined from their email archives, and asked them to distinguish between important and unimportant ones. The findings were striking. In spite of having huge archives of contacts (858 on average), participants rated only 14 percent (118) as important and worth keeping. Criteria for inclusion echoed those identified in our earlier interviews: Participants chose contacts with whom they interacted frequently and recently, and for a long time, and those who were likely to respond to their email messages. They excluded spammers.

Overall, interesting parallels appear among contacts, paper records, and email messages. People are exposed to many more contacts than they can record systematic information about, so they reserve judgment and overkeep data about contacts they may not need. Furthermore, the criteria people use to judge the value of contacts are based around usage and interaction. However, one key difference between email, paper records, and contacts is that a larger proportion of contacts are judged as unimportant by users.

Keeping Web Pages

Similar problematic keeping decisions also surface on the web (Jones 2004), where we see errors of *commission* (overkeeping information that turns out to have little future value) and *omission* (failing to keep information that turns out to be needed later). There are clear errors of commission; for example, people expend energy creating bookmarks that they never subsequently use. Tauscher and Greenberg (1997) showed that 58 percent of bookmarks are never used, suggesting poor decision making.

At the same time, other studies of web behaviors reveal failures of omission, cases in which people do not preserve information that turns out to be useful later. Wen (2003) coined the term *post retrieval value* to describe web resources that people have accessed but not preserved—only later realizing their utility. His study showed that people were able to later find only about 20 percent of information they had previously accessed and attended to in an earlier information retrieval session.

Keeping Photos

With the advent of digital photography, the number of pictures that people take has increased massively (Bentley, Metcalf, and Harboe 2006; Kirk et al. 2006; Whittaker, Bergman, and Clough 2010; Wilhelm et al. 2004). Similar keeping issues arise for digital photos as for other media. We looked at how and why people keep digital photos in a study of parents with young families (Whittaker, Bergman, and Clough 2010), who had an average of 4,475 digital pictures. All participants deleted some pictures, both when pictures were taken and when they were uploaded from camera to computer. Participants estimated they deleted on average 17 percent of their pictures. The reasons they gave for deletion were that the pictures were of poor technical quality or did not capture an event of interest. In general, deletion was a difficult process, as evidenced by the fact that many of the pictures that were kept were near duplicates (i.e., multiple pictures of identical scenes), an observation that is confirmed in other studies (Kirk et al. 2006). This suggests that people reserve their options about the best view of a given scene. One of the reasons people gave for such overkeeping was that they perceived little cost in keeping many photos. Therefore, they were not focused on the exploitation or retrieval context when they made keeping decisions. As with paper and email, people had a strong expectation that they would return to their photo collections at a later date to rationalize them and weed out extraneous photos. As in our paper and email studies, this rationalization seldom occurred.

Summary

Keeping decisions are difficult because they require people to (1) predict their future retrieval needs, (2) take into account the possibility that those information needs may change, and (3) make utility decisions under conditions of information overload, often basing judgments on incomplete readings of new information.

Errors are made, and the primary tendency is to overkeep—conservatively keeping things that are never accessed later. Overkeeping is observed with paper, email, contacts, and photo archives. There is also evidence from some web studies of the opposite tendency—that is, people failing to keep information that later turns out to be relevant.

Consistent with overkeeping, deletion is relatively infrequent, varying from 17 percent for photos to 30 percent for email messages. Contacts are different, however; it seems that because people are exposed to so many contacts, they regard the majority of those they encounter (86 percent) as unimportant.

The nature of the information item affects the keeping decision. This decision is relatively straightforward for certain items: We obviously need to keep actionable email messages that have not been handled or unique, personally generated items that no one else will safeguard. However, it is hard for people to determine the value of data such as public web pages or informative email messages.

Rather than viewing keeping as a one-time decision, people often use a deferral strategy—waiting to see whether information turns out to be useful. Two major weaknesses of deferral are that (1) people seldom return to their collections to carry out a reevaluation of tentatively kept information and (2) deferral means that collections are full of items of dubious value, which makes it more difficult to find truly valuable information.

People do not generally seem to be aware of the implications of overkeeping. Although they complain about how full their inboxes are, they nevertheless delete only 30 percent of email messages—and even after spending days working though paper archives, they still preserve 78 percent of the same. On the web, in contrast, there is a suggestion that people do not bookmark because they are aware that doing so will make valued materials harder to find. This could be because they consider web information to be unimportant or because they think it is easily recoverable by other means.

3 Management

Management is at the heart of curation. By actively imposing order on kept items, users increase their ability to retrieve those items in the future. We first describe different semantic and temporal strategies for organizing information. Then, we discuss factors that influence users' choice of management strategies and evaluate the trade-offs between these strategies. Finally, we talk briefly about a radical alternative that proposes we forgo active organization altogether and rely totally on search for information exploitation. We defer a full discussion here; chapter 5 describes studies that systematically evaluate this alternative, finding a strong preference for active organization, and chapter 8 seeks to explain this preference.

Management is a crucial curation process because it directly affects exploitation. We are constantly acquiring information. As a result, large amounts of personal information accumulate over long periods (Whittaker and Hirschberg 2001; Marshall 2008a, 2008b; Whittaker et al. 2002; Whittaker and Sidner 1996; Whittaker et al. 2011). Using current estimates of how many documents, digital photos, and email messages we acquire on a daily basis (Boardman and Sasse 2004; Whittaker, Bergman, and Clough 2010; Whittaker et al. 2011; Whittaker, Bellotti, and

Gwizdka 2007), and making the conservative estimate that these will remain constant over our fifty-year digital lifetimes, we will actively save around one hundred thousand documents, 440,000 email messages, and 120,000 digital photographs.

Certain types of management take place more often than we might expect. For certain items, such as files and email messages, people are perpetually and actively engaged in reorganization, as reflected by the frequent small modifications they make to the organization of their information. For example, a longitudinal study (Boardman and Sasse 2004) found that people create a new file folder every three days and make a new email folder every five days. In each case, the addition of a new structure demonstrates that people are constantly reflecting on how their information is currently organized and finding it to be inadequate. However, as described in chapter 2, people seldom engage in major reorganizations or extensive deletion. Instead, they tend to modify existing structures incrementally. In addition, different types of information are managed differently, and people are highly unlikely to monitor and reorganize photos for reasons that will become clear later in this chapter.

People also make management mistakes. They often engage in counterproductive behaviors when organizing their information. Studies of web bookmarking show that people construct complex hierarchical bookmarking systems (Abrams, Baecker, and Chignell 1998; Aula, Jhaveri, and Kaki 2005). However, we have seen that users never access 42 percent of the bookmarks they organize for later retrieval (Tauscher and Greenberg 1997). Efforts at organizing email messages also may not bear fruit. Email filing accounts for 10 percent of total time in email (Bellotti et al. 2005), yet information is usually accessed by browsing the inbox or searching, rather than via folder access (Tang et al.

2008; Whittaker 2005; Whittaker, Bellotti, and Gwizdka 2007; Whittaker et al. 2011). With personal photos, people may make the opposite type of mistake and fail to organize information when there is a clear need to do so. Later in this chapter we will review a study of personal photo retrieval that shows a failure to impose even rudimentary organization—in part because people believe that they will be able to retrieve their photos without needing to organize them (Whittaker, Bergman, and Clough 2010).

We will now discuss two fundamentally different types of organization that people apply to their personal files. The first type is semantic: information items are structured according to conceptual similarity. The second is temporal: it concerns reminding for actionable items, and the goal is to organize these items according to when they have to be processed.

As we discuss management, it may occur to the reader that emerging machine learning technologies such as facial recognition may affect how people will manage data such as photos. However we defer discussion until chapter 13 where we review emerging PIM technologies, because as yet we know of no studies that have empirically evaluated the impact of automatic photo classification on users' management behavior. For the same reasons, we postpone examination of techniques such as Inbox by Gmail that aim to manage actionable information using deferral.

Semantic Cueing

Semantic organization is a fundamental human cognitive activity. Even newborn infants categorize objects, with natural psychological categories tending to be based around exemplars or prototypes. For example, an individual's concept of *bird* is based heavily on common exemplars such as robins or blackbirds, rather than unusual cases such as penguins or ostriches. Our judgments and reasoning about categories are influenced by the extent to which particular instances are similar to those exemplars, with category exceptions and anomalies being more difficult to reason about (Rosch 1978; Rosch et al. 1976).

Most psychology research on organization has looked at natural categories—that is, how we mentally organize places, events, names, and faces. It has not looked at the types of information we are addressing here—that is, *synthetic*, human-generated information, such as documents, email messages, photos, or web pages. Nevertheless, considerable human–computer interaction (HCI) and information management research has looked into people's preferences for organizing such synthetic personal data. For example, as we will discuss in chapter 5, people prefer to organize and retrieve their documents spatially rather than by using keyword search (Barreau and Nardi 1995; Bergman et al. 2008). However, there are limits to the utility of spatial organization: Semantic labels are stronger retrieval cues than spatial organization alone, although combinations of semantic and spatial organization can enhance performance (Jones and Dumais 1986). In addition, semantic and spatial cues are enhanced when they are *self-selected*, rather than being chosen by an external party (Bergman, Beyth-Marom, and Nachmias 2003; Lansdale and Edmonds 1992), a finding we return to when we discuss shared repositories and group information management in chapter 7.

When managing personal information, two different and separate aspects of organization are important for effective exploitation: *mental cueing* and *external cueing*.

Mental cueing: As many psychological studies have shown, the mental act of imposing organization on information makes it inherently more memorable. Organizing things within a consistent conceptual structure means that, at recall, remembering one item from that structure may trigger memory of a related one; therefore, applying semantic organization is highly effective in promoting recall (Baddeley 1997; Craik and Lockhart 1972). Imposing organization on newly encountered information helps recall even if people do not have direct access to their organizational schemes at retrieval. For example, in a recent study, we showed that the simple act of organizing conversational information by taking structured notes increased recall, even when people did not use their notes at retrieval time (Kalnikaité and Whittaker 2008a).

External cueing: A second, more critical aspect of organization for PIM is that the products of organizational efforts can themselves be used as external retrieval cues. Seeing well-chosen folder names can cue people about folder contents and organization. Scanning the contents of a folder can also remind people of where related information is stored, and related information can itself serve to remind people of where a target file is located (Jones and Dumais 1986; Jones, Phuwanartnurak, et al. 2005; Lansdale 1988). If we write down and then later look at study notes, this can trigger our memory of information that we might otherwise have forgotten (Kalnikaité and Whittaker 2007, 2008a). It is also important to contrast these cueing processes with search. Users who have not actively organized files but rely instead on search do not have access to such mental and external cues at retrieval. They have to generate search terms from scratch, which is less accurate than cued recall (Mandler 1980;

Neisser 2014). Search also requires different, more demanding cognitive processes, as we will explain in chapter 8.

While mental and external cueing processes are often successful in promoting retrieval, such success is not guaranteed. Human memory is highly context dependent, with successful long-term retrieval being reliant on reconstructing the specific context in which information was first remembered (Tulving and Thomson 1973). Choosing appropriate folder organization and labels therefore requires people to predict exactly how they will be thinking about particular information at the time that they need to retrieve it. Predicting future retrieval context is difficult, because there are usually multiple ways that a file can be categorized, such as by author, topic, date or project. The inability to accurately predict how one will think about information in the future makes it more likely that future retrieval will fail.

Organization and labeling are mainstays of most computer operating systems. The primary way people organize their digital information is to sort it into categories (in directories, folders, or subfolders) and then apply meaningful labels to these folders and subfolders. Following common usage, we refer to these nested folders as *hierarchies*. The previously mentioned cognitive studies (Baddeley 1997; Craik and Lockhart 1972; Jones, Phuwanartnurak, et al. 2005; Kalnikaité and Whittaker 2008a; Lansdale 1988) suggest that the act of applying folder organization may help retrieval in two ways: first, by mental cueing; and second, by generating a navigable conceptual structure, with folder labels serving as external retrieval cues. Note also that folders usually contain a strong spatial component, with subfolders sitting inside folders; this too can help cue retrieval (Jones and Dumais 1986). We return to the importance of location in chapter 8, in which we explore cognitive and neurological mechanisms underlying virtual folder navigation.

Temporal Cueing

Temporal organization is a second, less obvious type of organization that has been less extensively researched in PIM. It promotes temporal cueing. We have already seen that much important information people deal with is actionable, and it is usually the case that those actions are required to happen by a certain time—for example, to meet a certain deadline. This leads us to the problem of reminding (Sellen et al. 1997). It does no good to have an extensive organizational structure that allows access to any item if you forget the deadline relating to that information. Reminding is a critical PIM problem—especially in the case of email, in which actionable items are prevalent.

There is also evidence for the utility of temporal organization as a retrieval cue. People can successfully retrieve documents by associating them with personal or public events ("landmarks") that occurred close to when the documents were encountered or created (Ringel et al. 2003). This is similar to retrieval processes that take place in human autobiographical memory,—that is, our memory of personally experienced events. Although people are poor at determining the absolute time when an event occurred, they are much better at locating target events relative to such salient landmark events (Wagenaar 1986). The importance of temporal factors is also shown by analyzing logfiles that trace people's online searches and file retrievals. These logfiles reveal a bias toward retrieval of highly recent information (Cutrell et al. 2006; Dumais et al. 2003; Fitchett, Cockburn, and Gutwin 2013).

In addition to these overall organizational preferences, other work has explored different types of management strategies and what motivates people to choose them. We will now describe such strategies for paper, digital files, email, web documents, and photos. We will review the types of management strategies employed, what influences people's choice of strategy, and the trade-offs between strategies. Again, note that although the focus of this book is on digital curation, we will also review studies of how people organize paper, because those studies illustrate management principles that generalize across media.

Managing Paper

Malone (1983) conducted a pioneering study into people's organizational habits for paper, identifying two main strategies he called filing and piling. *Filing* involves constructing an exhaustive, hierarchical taxonomy, with labels for each (sub)category and semantically related items stored in each category. In contrast, *piling* is more laissez-faire, usually resulting in less systematic organization with no substructure. Piles tend to be fewer in number, and each pile contains more items; looser associations exist between items stored in the same pile, with items organized by the sequence in which they were acquired. Items may also be in a common pile because they were generated or acquired at the same time. Piles are often used for actionable information and reminding.

There are clear trade-offs between these two organizational strategies. Piles are easier to create and maintain because they are less systematic. They have a less clear organizational structure with more items in each pile, which may make retrieval within each pile less efficient. However, because there tend to be fewer piles in total, this system leaves fewer potential locations from which to retrieve, which may compensate for the lack of organization. Piles are typically sorted in chronological order, with more recent papers on top of older ones. This promotes incidental finding of recent information that is on top; a user is reminded of its existence and of the task relating to it. Having a small number of piles may also mean that users visit each pile more frequently and as a result may become more familiar with the contents of each. However, Malone also found that piles don't scale well and are difficult to scan if they contain huge numbers of items. Papers put at the top of piles for reminding become buried under more recent papers, making them difficult to retrieve. In contrast, filing via labeled ring binders requires more effort at creation time and more maintenance, but the binders offer benefits at retrieval, providing a more coherent retrieval structure and more relevant labels that serve as external cues. These advantages may be offset by the fact that paper files may contain many subcategories, leaving many levels to navigate. Files may also fall into disrepair, with too many levels/distinctions being too infrequently visited, making differences between categories harder to remember in email archives (Whittaker and Sidner 1996).

In the office move study described previously (Whittaker and Hirschberg 2001), we investigated when and why people choose filing or piling strategies. The distinction between filers and pilers was not absolute, being instead one of degree. All our respondents filed some information but kept other information in desktop piles. We classified users according to how likely they were to file information. Based on the predominant strategies that people described in our interviews, we identified a threshold of 40 percent to categorize people as filers.

Pilers often amassed information without attempting to organize it systematically. This laissez-faire approach should have led to an accumulation of unscrutinized information before the office move—but we found to our surprise that pilers had smaller original archives. They also had less preserved information than filers after cleaning out their archives. Why then did filers amass more information? Our interviews suggested one possible reason is *premature filing*. As we saw in chapter 2, people often acquire information that turns out to be of little utility that must be discarded later. If filers are more likely to incorporate documents of uncertain quality into their filing systems, we might expect them to throw away more reference materials than pilers while preparing for the move. This was not true for all documents, but was true for reference documents.

There were also differences between the two strategies in terms of data acquisition and management. We expected pilers to acquire information faster because they tend not to scrutinize incoming data as carefully. We looked at data acquisition rates in separate analyses of original and preserved (i.e., post-move) information volumes. For both measures, pilers tended to be slower to acquire both original and preserved information. It may be that acquisition rates are affected by differences in frequency of access between piles and files. Because there are fewer piles overall, it may be that piles are revisited more often, leading pilers to detect and discard more irrelevant information. In contrast, because files are less frequently accessed, people may be less likely to cull irrelevant information.

Given their more systematically organized systems, we expected filers to have an easier time finding data and that they would access their data more often. Contrary to our expectations, pilers accessed a greater percentage of documents than filers over the previous year. Why were pilers more likely to access recent data? Interviews revealed that both strategies had strengths and weaknesses. With a piling strategy, information is more accessible: It can be located in a relatively small number of piles through which people frequently sift. The result is that valuable, frequently accessed information moves to the top of the piles, and less relevant material is located lower down. This pattern of repeated access allows people to identify important information, discarding unused or irrelevant information. A different reason that filers may access proportionally less of their data is simply that they have more stuff. There are finite constraints on how much data one can access. Filers have more data, and as a consequence they are able to access less of it. This is consistent with the observation that the absolute amounts of data accessed by both groups were very similar.

The lack of a coherent system in piling does have some disadvantages. Taken to excess, piles can dominate not only working surfaces but all areas of the office, and large piles are highly laborious to scan. However, even though filing is more systematic, it does not always guarantee easy access to information. With complex data, filing systems can become so arcane that people forget the categories they have previously created, leading to duplicate categories. Accessing only one of these duplicates leads to incomplete retrieval because some part of the original information has been overlooked. This illustrates a general disadvantage to filing strategies: They incur a large overhead for constructing, maintaining, and rationalizing complex organizations of documents. Similar trade-offs between simple and more exhaustive organizational schemes are reported in a study comparing folders and tags as methods of organizing personal information (Civan et al. 2008).

We also expected filers to be quicker to rationalize their data in preparing for the move, given the greater care they had initially taken to organize their data—but in fact, there were no differences in packing time between filers and pilers. This could be because filers' greater organization is offset by having more data through which to sift. Contrary to our predictions, pilers found it subjectively easier to rationalize archives in preparation for the move. Why was this? Even though filers discarded more reference information, they generally found it difficult to discard filed documents, partly because of the investment they had already made in managing that information. That is, filers seemed less disposed to discard information they had invested effort in organizing. In contrast, unfiled information seemed easier to discard.

Finally, we looked at what determined strategy choice. Although job type influenced strategy somewhat (e.g., secretaries were more likely to be filers), in general strategy seemed to be more affected by dispositional factors. We return to this point later in our discussion of PIM and personality.

Managing Digital Files and Folders

We access our files and folders on a daily basis, and their organization has clear importance for our everyday digital lives—yet there have been relatively few explorations of how people organize these files and what influences this organization. One exception is Boardman and Sasse's 2004 study, in which they found that people had on average fifty-seven folders, with a depth of 3.3 folders. The study also documented different filing strategies, finding that 58 percent of people systematically filed information items when they created them, a further 35 percent left many items unfiled in default locations such as My Documents (in a manner similar to paper piling), and a small proportion (6 percent) left most items unfiled. However, in a large-scale study involving 296 participants (Bergman et al. 2010), we found that people tend to file the large majority of their files in folders that they personally created, leaving only 12 percent of files in default folders (e.g., My Documents). In some cases, Boardman and Sasse (2004) found that people did not file actionable documents (i.e., those they were currently working on), instead leaving them in obvious places—such as the computer desktop—where they would trigger reminding. Boardman and Sasse also looked longer term to see whether management strategies showed large-scale changes over time, but found little evidence for this.

Two other studies explored the structure of people's file systems. Gonçalves and Jorge (2003) studied the folder structures of eleven computer scientists using various operating systems: eight using Windows, two using Linux, and one using Solaris. Their results show extremely deep, narrow hierarchies. The average directory depth was 8.45, with an average *branching factor*—an estimation of the mean number of subfolders per folder—of 1.84, indicating a deep and narrow hierarchy. In contrast, a larger-scale study by Henderson and Srinivasan (2009) looked at the folder structures of seventy-three university employees using Windows OS. The structures they found were much shallower, being only 3.4 folders deep on average. Folders tended to be broader, with an average of 4.1 subfolders per folder for folders that contain subfolders. Both studies found relatively small numbers of files per folder: thirteen for Gonçalves and Jorge (2003) and 11.1 for Henderson and Srinivasan (2009). Our own large-scale study observed shallow and but wide folder hierarchies, with an average depth of 2.86 folders and 10.64 sub-folders per folder (Bergman et al. 2010). We will discuss this latter study in more detail in chapter 4. Our study is unique because it not only analyzes folder structure but also tests the effect of this structure on retrieval.

In another study probing why people generate specific folder structures, Jones, Phuwanartnurak, et al. (2005) interviewed people about the nature of their folder systems. Consistent with external cueing (i.e., when folder and file names serve as memory prompts), many folders were seen as *plans*—structures that people used to organize their future work. Folders represented the main tasks and subtasks of ongoing projects, serving to remind people about aspects of their work activity that need to be executed. People also used workarounds to make various types of information more salient—for example, labeling folders "aacurrent" instead of "current" to ensure that important information was more obvious, rising to the top when browsing an alphabetically ordered folder list. This is an example of information promotion that manipulates the salience of important information, which we discuss in chapter 10.

Users also repeatedly access their files, often multiple times per day. One implication of such continual reaccess is that users are likely to discover suboptimal organization, leading them to modify their file and folder structures. Interestingly, Jones, Phuwanartnurak, et al. (2005) also found that people organize their folders over time in an ad hoc, bottom-up fashion as relationships emerged between files: When users observed that several files related to the same category, they created a new subfolder for that category and moved the related files to it. Adaptive maintenance and modification will turn out to be important when, later in this chapter, we discuss archives that are much less frequently accessed, which often prove to be poorly structured.

More recently, new tools have been developed to support different types of organization. One example is *tagging*, which allows users to apply multiple labels to a given information item, rather than storing it in a single folder location. Tagging has several intuitive advantages. It potentially provides richer external retrieval cues (because multiple labels are available as retrieval terms), and it allows users to filter sets of retrieved items in terms of their tagged properties (e.g., entering "pictures + personal" returns files with those tags). Tagging also does not require users to place items in a single unique storage location that may be hard to remember. However, in chapter 6 we will review multiple lab studies comparing tagging and foldering that fail to find definitive benefits for tags. We then describe our own work, which indicates that people prefer folders to tags for both management and retrieval. Even when people use tags, they rarely exploit multiple classification.

Managing Email

Managing email is complex, and different from paper or standard digital files. As we have seen, a critical aspect of email is that it contains many actionable messages. To be effective, people need to organize actionable information in such a way that they are reminded of what they need to do and when. In this section, we first describe how users process actionable messages and then turn to what they do with informative messages. One important insight is that the email inbox is often treated like a pile in which actionable messages are not actively organized but are kept highly available for reminding. In contrast, email folders are generally used for informative messages that users have actively classified into files. Again, note that although some of these studies are almost twenty years old, many of the problems they identify—such as remembering actionable emails—are still very much with us. These problems remain despite email technology undergoing quite fundamental changes during that period.

Actionable Messages

For actionable items, deferral is inevitable. As our discussion of keeping illustrated, only a small proportion of actionable messages can be dealt with at once; most must wait to be processed. Forgetting these deferred tasks can create major headaches both for the user and the organization. Whittaker and Sidner (1996) found that the most prevalent strategy for being reminded about actionable messages is to leave them in the inbox. Users know that they will return to the inbox to access incoming unprocessed messages and hope also to be reminded about their outstanding actionable messages. We called this strategy *no filing*.

Some of the users in our study experimented with other strategies for managing actionable data, but these were unsuccessful. For example, 25 percent of users filed actionable items in a to-do folder. Whittaker and Sidner dubbed these people *frequent filers*. There are obvious advantages to frequent filing: Removing items from the inbox keeps it trim, allowing users to focus on new and important information. However, in 95 percent of cases, the to-do folder was abandoned because it did not provide opportunistic reminding. Instead, using a to-do folder meant that people had to explicitly remember to go to that folder and review its contents. These additional steps are a clear deterrent that prevents most users from using to-do folders, although other studies (Bellotti et al. 2003) suggest that some users will change their work practices to exploit them.

Of course, there are also disadvantages to leaving actionable items in the inbox: Such reminders may be difficult to spot if the user receives many new messages that displace older, pending actionable items—requiring users continually to scroll through the inbox to ensure that these items are not out of sight and out of mind (Whittaker 2005; Whittaker, Jones, and Terveen 2002; Whittaker and Sidner 1996). Tang and colleagues (2008) looked at the proportion of the inbox that users constantly had visible, finding that on average only 25 percent of inbox messages were in view. More recent email clients, such as Gmail and Outlook, allow users to flag messages using "stars" to make certain messages more visible. However, as we discuss in part III, such flagging is still dependent on having relatively few marked messages in order to allow flags to be visible.

A final strategy for organizing actionable items is a hybrid, combining use of the inbox with occasional filing. Whittaker and Sidner (1996) identified a final group accounting for 35 percent of their users; these users engaged in *spring cleaning*. Such users wait until huge amounts of information accumulate in their inboxes, making it hard to identify actionable items. Then, they engage in extensive filing to rationalize the inbox. The process repeats, with the inbox gradually growing in size until another crisis brings on another extensive filing bout.

What determines people's strategy choice for processing actionable email messages? Whittaker and Sidner (1996) examined whether organizational role or incoming volume of messages affected processing strategy. Although managers received greater volumes of email, there was no evidence of a direct relationship between strategy and role. As with paper and computer filing, it may be that dispositional factors are an important determinant of strategy choice (Massey et al., 2014). Indeed other research has demonstrated relations between cognitive style and strategy (Gwizdka 2004a, 2004b).

Other studies of email found support for these three management strategies of filing, no filing, and spring cleaning (Bellotti et al. 2005; Dabbish et al. 2005; Fisher et al. 2006; Whittaker 2005; Whittaker, Jones, and Terveen 2002). However, later work extended these initial categories, suggesting that there are few pure "no filer" instances; even users who mainly rely on their inboxes for task management still create a few folders. Bälter (2000) also proposed a temporal progression between different strategies as people receive more email. He argued that people move sequentially from being frequent filers to being spring cleaners, and later to being no filers as the volume of email they receive increases. Bälter's argument is that those receiving the highest volumes of email have the least time to organize it.

Informative Messages

Now, we'll look at how users organize informative messages. Users do experience problems in processing informative email messages. Recall that on average 10 percent of people's total time in email is spent filing messages (Bellotti et al. 2005). Although users of more modern email clients now rely on somewhat rudimentary filing (Fisher et al. 2006), for many users filing is still important (Whittaker et al. 2011).

Again, Whittaker and Sidner (1996) examined why users have problems with filing informative messages. Filing is hard for several reasons. Generating and maintaining folder collections requires considerable effort, and success is highly dependent on being able to envisage future retrieval requirements. As we saw in chapter 2, some people use the *deferral strategy*. They postpone filing until they have a better idea about how they might organize information.

Our own data (Whittaker and Sidner 1996) show that email filing often fails. Research combining multiple studies shows that people have an average of around thirty-nine email folders (Whittaker, Bellotti, and Gwizdka 2007). Whittaker and Sidner (1996) found that on average, 35 percent of email folders contain only one or two items. These tiny folders may be too small to be useful. A major aim of filing is to coerce the huge number of undifferentiated informative inbox items into a relatively small set of folders, each containing multiple related messages. Filing clearly is not successful if the number of messages in a given folder is small. Later studies duplicated these observations, but found a lower percentage (16 percent) of such failed folders (Fisher et al. 2006). These tiny failed folders do not significantly reduce the complexity of the inbox; moreover, they introduce the dual overheads of (1) creating folders in the first place and (2) remembering multiple folder definitions every time there is a decision to make about filing a new inbox item. The cost of creating too many folders is illustrated by the fact that the larger the number of folders a user has, the more likely that person is to generate failed folders containing only one or two items (Whittaker and Sidner 1996). Of course, a small number of these failed folders may represent new activities that the user is planning (Jones, Phuwanartnurak, et al. 2005), but such planning cannot account for all of these tiny folders.

Folders can also fail because they are too big. When there are too many messages in a folder, it becomes unwieldy and difficult to scan (Bergman et al. 2010). As the relationships among messages within the folder become more tenuous, the benefit of keeping them together is much reduced. With large, heterogeneous folders, it can be extremely difficult to collate related items or to find a target item (Bergman et al. 2010; Whittaker and Sidner 1996).

Elsweiler, Baillie, and Ruthven (2008) looked at the impact of filing strategy on users' memories of their email messages. Frequent filers tended to remember less about their email messages. This is consistent with our earlier observations about premature filing. Filing information too quickly can lead to the creation of archives containing spurious information; quick filing also means that users are not exposed to the information frequently in the inbox, making it hard to remember the information's properties or even its existence.

Thus, email users experience cognitive difficulties in creating folders for informative messages. In addition, the payoffs for this effort may not be great: Folders can be too large, too small, or too numerous for people to remember individual folder definitions. In consequence, folders may be of restricted use either for retrieval or for collating related messages. As we have seen, some users finesse this problem: instead of filing informative messages, they leave many of them in their inbox. Clients such as Gmail try to support this strategy by introducing thread-based viewers that collate related messages. Threaded viewers allow related messages to be dealt with together and can reduce the size of the inbox.

Managing Web Pages

Unlike email, web information largely is not actionable: Users may want to ensure that they remember to read a web page, but in general there are no negative consequences for failing to do so.

One prevalent form of managing web information is to bookmark encountered web pages. Numerous older studies have looked into how people organize their bookmarks. Two early studies documented both the number of bookmarks created and their underlying structure. For example, Abrams, Baecker, and Chignell (1998) found that 68 percent of respondents had between eleven and one hundred bookmarks, and Boardman and Sasse (2004) found that people organized their bookmarks into an average of seventeen folders. Another study (Bruce, Jones, and Dumais 2004) observed further strategies people use for organizing useful web information. These other strategies were heterogeneous. In addition to bookmarking, users might forward themselves a link in email, print the page, copy the link into a document, generate a sticky note, or rely on memory.

More recent work with modern web browsers has revisited bookmarking. Aula, Jhaveri, and Kaki (2005) looked at people's bookmark collections and found that 92 percent of people use bookmarks, with an average of 220 links, although there is huge individual variation: 21 percent of people have fewer than fifty bookmarks, and 6 percent have none. The largest collection contained 2,589 links and 425 folders. Most of the study's informants reported major problems in organizing and managing their bookmark collections. Consistent with early studies (Tauscher and Greenberg 1997), bookmark organization sometimes failed; users often bookmarked information that they never subsequently revisited. In contrast, other studies showed that users were unwilling to create new bookmarks, fearing that creating bookmarks for information of unclear utility would clutter their existing set of useful bookmarks—and thus compromise the utility of useful items (Aula, Jhaveri, and Kaki 2005; Wen 2003).

Aula, Jhaveri, and Kaki (2005) also found that success with complex bookmark collections depends on whether users actively exploit and maintain their collection of links. A subgroup of heavy users of bookmarks had collections of over five hundred links; these users tended (like email spring cleaners) to reorganize their collections periodically, deleting unused or no longer functioning links. They also carefully organized bookmarks into hierarchical levels (similar to a file system). For these users who invested organizational effort, bookmarks seemed to be an indispensable tool. Abrams, Baecker, and Chignell (1998) also looked at the types of strategies people used for organizing their bookmarks. They found four main types: About 50 percent of people were sporadic filers, a further 26 percent never organized bookmarks into folders, around 23 percent created folders when they accessed a web page, and around 7 percent created folders at the end of a session. Creating folders also seems to be a response to having too many bookmarks in a dropdown list; people with fewer than thirty-five bookmarks have no folders, but beyond this threshold folders grow linearly with the number of bookmarks.

Some disadvantages of bookmarking relate to the costs of creating and maintaining collections, especially as users' information needs change. Web 2.0 social tagging systems—such as Delicious, Dogear, Onomi, and Citeulike—finesse some of these problems. These social tagging systems allow users to create multiple labels for the same data, providing potentially richer retrieval cues (Cutrell et al. 2006; Lansdale 1988). More importantly, they allow tags to be shared among users, reducing the cost of tag creation for each user. Of course, this collaborative approach raises important questions, which we revisit in more detail in chapter 7. Do different users agree on a common classification of information, or do they generate inconsistent, orthogonal labels? Numerous studies have shown that, given sufficient numbers of users, shared tag sets tend to stabilize on consistent web page labels so that people can exploit others' tags (Golder and Huberman 2006; Millen et al. 2007). Furthermore, suitable user interface designs (e.g., text completion) can address problems such as inconsistent spellings and promote greater awareness of others' tags (Millen et al. 2007). If enough people are prepared to tag, social tagging seems a useful tool that removes some of the costs associated with standard, individual bookmarking methods. However, these results are dependent on achieving a critical mass of active tags. As we will see in chapter 6, tagging is less efficient and less commonly used when it is enacted by a single person.

Managing Photos

Photos are very different from email messages and web pages, tending to be self-generated (like many personal files), and are usually neither informative nor actionable. Instead, they often generate strong affective responses (Frohlich et al. 2002). They are also perceived to be highly important and often irreplaceable (Petrelli, Whittaker, and Brockmeier 2008; Whittaker, Bergman, and Clough 2010). How, then, do people organize them? Recent studies show that people manage photos using rather rudimentary structures (Kirk et al. 2006; Whittaker, Bergman, and Clough 2010).

Whittaker, Bergman, and Clough (2010) investigated how parents organized their family photo archives. They found that these collections tended to have very little hierarchical structure and were organized more like piles than files. Participants typically relied on a single main picture storage location (such as the My Pictures folder). Participants with multiple computers or external hard drives usually had a single main storage folder on each device. People usually stored their pictures in that location in a single-level, flat hierarchy with minimal subfolders. Furthermore, these pile-like folders often contained heterogeneous data, comprising pictures that related to multiple events, possibly because they were uploaded at the same time and never subsequently reorganized.

How can we explain this lack of systematic organization? Previous work has highlighted how participants are able to exploit their familiarity with *recently taken* pictures to scan, sort, and organize them for sharing with others (Kirk et al. 2006). Possibly because of these successful experiences with recent pictures, people may expect themselves to be very familiar with their *entire* picture collection, regardless of its age. As a result, they may not see the need to organize their collections carefully. In most cases, it seemed that people in our study had not accessed the vast majority of their pictures since they were uploaded. We saw evidence of such infrequent access during retrieval. Participants universally preferred to view pictures in the thumbnail view for easier visual scanning. If participants had previously opened these folders, we would have expected to see thumbnails. Yet during retrieval, when participants first opened folders, photos almost always appeared in the "list" view (generally the default on most systems), suggesting folders had rarely been accessed. Because participants seldom access pictures, they may not discover how poorly organized they are. One reason for this lack of organization and unfamiliarity is that parents typically have very little spare time to organize their photos. One participant commented that his attitude to photos was "collect now, organize later, view in the future."

Another way to organize might be to annotate pictures by applying labels to describe their contents. However, consistent with earlier studies (Frohlich et al. 2002; Kirk et al. 2006; Rodden and Wood 2003), we found very little evidence of annotation. One reason is that annotating is onerous even for small picture collections and impractical for large ones. Another problem, also observed in earlier studies (Kirk et al. 2006; Rodden and Wood 2003), is that users may not annotate because they are unaware that they are likely to forget key aspects of pictures. People know they can remember detailed information about recent pictures, and this may mean they feel little motivation to annotate pictures to prepare for the eventuality that they will forget. However, the final chapter of this book discusses new systems that automatically label photos using facial recognition methods, although as we will see, these systems will not solve annotation problems overnight.

Individual Differences and Personality Traits in Management

Individual differences are prevalent in PIM (Gwizdka 2004a, 2004b; Gwizdka and Chignell 2007). There is large variation between individuals in how they structure information in personal archives. These differences make it hard to develop general PIM tools. However, we know little about the origins of these differences. Various studies have proposed that job type influences management strategy, but this relationship has not been clearly demonstrated (Whittaker and Sidner 1996; Whittaker and Hirschberg 2001). Another possibility is that differences relate to individual traits. Massey et al. (2014) describe two studies that evaluated whether management differences arise from underlying personality traits by exploring whether different personality types organize personal file collections differently. The first exploratory study asked participants to identify PIM cues that signal personality traits. Participants were given a view of someone's file system and asked to infer that person's personality. Participants also identified which organizational cues informed those inferences; for example, many participants took complex folders and subfolders as indications that the file system owner had a Conscientious personality. Although the aim was to identify potential cues, these cues also proved surprisingly accurate indicators of personality.

In a second study to evaluate these cues, Massey et al. (2014) directly measured relations between file system structure and personality traits. We profiled each participant's file system to determine key structural properties, including total number of files, number of folders, and average files per folder, as well as other properties, such as number of music and photo files, among others. Next, we administered a standard personality survey to the file system owner in order to classify the owner according to the standard personality traits of Openness, Conscientiousness, Extraversion, Agreeableness, and Neuroticism (John 1990). Then, we examined relationships among structural properties of each file system and its owner's personality traits. There were important differences in file organization that related to personality traits. We found that Conscientiousness predicts file organization, particularly how PC users organize their desktops. Conscientious people were less likely to keep unorganized information on their PC desktops. Neurotic people keep more unorganized files on their PC desktops and may also keep more desktop files overall.

Summary

Management is a difficult activity, because it requires people to predict when or how information will be accessed. To create effective organization, users have to anticipate the context in which they will be accessing information. For action-oriented items, they have to anticipate exactly when they will need those items.

Information properties have a major impact on management strategy: Actionable items often require deferral, so people need to be reminded about them. Various tracking strategies facilitate reminding, including leaving actionable information in one's workspace as well as using dedicated task folders. There are trade-offs between these strategies: Keeping information in a workspace affords constant reminding, but it reduces efficiency, because that workspace can become cluttered with many unrelated actionable items. The disadvantage of dedicated to-do folders is that they need to be accessed and monitored deliberately.

For informative items, people use two main strategies: filing and piling. There are surprising advantages of using a paper piling strategy. As long as the collection is small, it seems to allow easy access to information items sorted chronologically into small numbers of piles. However, piles may not be efficient as the collection grows. Filing can also be problematic. Users often experience difficulty in categorizing information, failing to accurately predict the context in which they will retrieve that information. People create folders that are both too big (containing large collections of heterogeneous items) and too small (containing one or two items in a folder that is seldom used). People can also create duplicate folders for the same content. In addition, we found problems with premature filing of low-value information, leading people to generate complex collections of information that are of little utility. All of these factors make filing an error-prone process.

Both users' dispositions and information overload may influence the type of organizational strategy people employ. Users who receive large volumes of incoming information are under pressure to keep their workspaces clear (otherwise they may overlook important deferred actionable items). Ironically, they are also the people who are least likely to have the time to file and organize their information.

Certain types of information, such as bookmarks and photos, are infrequently reaccessed. Infrequent access may mean that people fail to realize what information they have available and how poorly organized it is. Collaborative tags seem to have benefits in a web or intranet context, in which people can reduce the cost of annotation by sharing others' labels. However, the benefits of tagging are dependent on having a critical mass of people generate such labels.

4 Exploitation

In this chapter, we first contrast exploitation with classic information seeking and foraging behaviors. Next, we describe different strategies for exploitation as well as the costs and benefits of such strategies. We then discuss methods for studying retrieval and report on research regarding information retrieval for files, emails, photos, and web information.

Exploitation: Definition and Strategies

We have seen that exploitation is different from information foraging and information seeking behaviors studied in classic information science. In both foraging (Pirolli 2007; Pirolli and Card 1995) and information seeking (Belkin 1980; Marchionini 1995; Wilson 1999), the target information is *novel*; that is, the user is seeking information that is new to them. Exploitation of familiar personal information is different in several ways. First, retrieval structures are subjectively organized, rather than publicly generated. People are exploiting their own organization, not a public database. As a result, exploiters may remember significant details about target information items and how they are organized. As we have already noted, the process of actively organizing material increases memory for the material being organized (Craik and Lockhart 1972)—and appropriately chosen labels or folder names can serve as external cues to remind where information is located.

People do indeed remember a significant amount about their personal data. For example, Gonçalves and Jorge (2004) asked participants to tell stories about three personal documents on which they had recently worked. People could remember a great deal about these documents, with the most salient characteristics being age, location, and purpose of the document. Blanc-Brude and Scalpin (2007) also found strong recall of personal documents, with location, format, age, keywords, and associated events being frequently remembered. Because people remember such information, access is not purely reliant on publicly provided metadata (*scent*, in the terminology of information foraging). Instead, as we have seen, exploitation of personal information is mediated by *cueing*—and cues can be mental or external. Indeed, as we described in the previous chapter, the main goal of management activities is to construct personal organizations that trigger these cueing processes to promote successful future exploitation.

To create effective retrieval cues, users need to anticipate successfully *when* and *how* they will reaccess information. Exploitation success depends whether the cues/structures that users have generated to anticipate future retrieval match the actual context at the time of retrieval. If there is a good match between organizational cues and the retrieval context, retrieval will succeed.

To recap, we exploit personal information using two main strategies: *navigation* involves manual traversal and visual scanning within self-generated hierarchies of folders and subfolders.

In *search*, users generate queries that specify a property of the target item, and a desktop search engine returns a set of results from which the user selects a relevant item.

Retrieval Research Methods

It is much more difficult to study retrieval than organization. Organization can be directly observed, and researchers can measure structure at a certain point in time using dedicated software (Henderson and Srinivasan 2009; Gonçalves and Jorge 2003; Massey et al. 2014). Researchers can also learn about organization using a semistructured interview called the *guided tour*, in which participants guide an interviewer through their folders while explaining how they organize their information (Boardman and Sasse 2004; Kwasnik 1991; Malone 1983). Finally, researchers can observe changes in organization by viewing the folder organization at different points in time (Jones, Phuwanartnurak, et al. 2005). Retrievals, on the other hand, are brief events that occur unexpectedly throughout a participant's day, leaving few observable traces. Without installing invasive logging tools, a researcher is left with only the impractical option of looking over the participant's shoulder for hours waiting for retrieval to occur. How then can retrieval be studied?

One way to study retrieval is to give participants artificial information items to organize and then observe retrieval (e.g., Fitchett, Cockburn, and Gutwin 2013; Civan et al. 2008; Gao 2011; Pak, Pautz, and Iden 2007). This procedure has the advantages of a *controlled task*: the experimenter determines when and how information items are retrieved (instead of waiting for retrieval to occur). Furthermore, the experiment typically takes place in a lab, so all relevant variables can be recorded and mea-sured. However, this method lacks ecological validity. We have repeatedly observed that users are typically intimately familiar with their own information items and organization in PIM (Bergman, Beyth-Marom, and Nachmias 2003; Jones, Phuwan-artnurak, et al. 2005); therefore, accessing artificial information items may be unrepresentative of authentic retrievals.

In our own research, we addressed this problem by develop-ing a new research technique we called *elicited personal informa-tion retrieval* (EPIR). In this technique, to increase ecological validity the tester asks participants to retrieve sample files from their own personal information collections and using their own computers. However, EPIR retains the advantages of a controlled experiment, because the tester initiates the retrievals and mea-sures relevant variables by videotaping participants' computer screens—for example, to see how efficient and successful partici-pants are at retrieving their own files.

Of course, EPIR does not exactly replicate real-life retrieval, because it involves retrieval that is prompted by specifying a tar-get file name rather than the broader context of work in which files are typically retrieved. Two more naturalistic alternatives are to use *diaries* (Teevan et al. 2004) or *logfiles* (Whittaker et al. 2011) to record participants' spontaneous retrievals. However, diaries can be problematic. They are typically used in small-scale qualitative studies with limited external validity; participants report on their retrieval behavior after the event, and they may omit important information (e.g., retrieval time). Getting par-ticipants to reliably complete their diaries is also problematic. Logfiles are difficult to collect both for technical and privacy reasons. Therefore, they are typically used only when a new pro-totype is tested. In addition, there may be issues involved in interpreting exact user intentions from complex logfile data (Whittaker et al. 2011).

We used EPIR for the file navigation study described in the next section and for the subsequent section examining photo retrieval, as well as in chapter 7, when we studied collaborative file systems (GIM) from the retrieval perspective, and also in chapter 8, when we examined neurological bases of retrieval strategy choice. The section about email refinding in this chapter reports a logfile analysis.

Accessing Files

In chapter 3, we discussed multiple studies that explore different organizational strategies, including filing and piling. However, few studies have explicitly quantified the relationship between file system structure on the one hand and retrieval success and retrieval efficiency on the other. It seems, however, that there must be retrieval implications that follow from organizing files in different ways. One trade-off is between large versus small folders: Large folders lead to shallower hierarchies. They reduce the number of folders to be scanned, but increase the time to scan the contents of each folder. In contrast, smaller folders result in narrow, deep hierarchies that reduce scan time per folder, but more folders have to be accessed overall, and each step down the hierarchy path takes time and increases chances of error.

We explored these trade-offs in a large-scale study (Bergman et al. 2010). We asked 296 participants to retrieve a total of 1,131 of their active files and analyzed each of the 5,035 navigation steps in these retrievals. Participants used their own computers for the retrieval task. They began each retrieval from their desktops, and we videotaped each navigation sequence. This allowed us to observe the characteristics of each folder that participants accessed as they attempted to locate the target file. We were also able to determine other structural information, including the depth of the retrieved file in the user's folder hierarchy and how many other items were present at each level as users traversed down the file hierarchy.

Folder structures were generally found to be shallow: Active files were retrieved from a mean depth of 2.86 folders. Folders were also relatively small: They contained a mean of 11.82 files per folder along with multiple subfolders (*Mean (M)* = 10.64). Retrieval time and success depended on folder size and depth, but overall navigation was successful and efficient, with participants successfully accessing 94 percent of their files and taking just 14.76 seconds to do so on average. It therefore seems that users' decisions to exploit both shallow structure and relatively small folders are adaptive.

We used linear regression to develop a predictive model to quantify the effects of folder depth and folder size on retrieval time. The model suggests an optimization for the trade-off between folder size and depth. According to the model, each additional folder step increases retrieval time by 2.236 seconds, and each new information item added to a folder increases retrieval time by 0.106 seconds. The trade-off between depth and size is therefore 2.236/0.106 = 21.09. Each step down the hierarchy is equivalent to scanning about twenty-one information items in terms of its effect on retrieval time. Therefore, as a heuristic, we can recommend that users avoid storing more than twenty-one information items per folder; they should create an additional level of subfolders instead.

We also explored retrieval differences between Mac and PC as well as the effects of different default presentations on retrieval (Bergman, Whittaker, et al. 2012). Results showed differences in overall retrieval time between PC and Mac, which arise from different organizational strategies rather than interface design differences. Mac users are more likely to create shallower folder hierarchies than PC users. We also found that the default Windows presentation is suboptimal: Users are quickest to retrieve information when their default explorer view shows icons. This is important because if this default were changed, retrieval time would be reduced substantially.

Accessing Email

Accessing information in email is a critical problem given the amount of time that people spend processing it and the fact that email serves both as a to-do list for actionable information and as an archive for informative data (Ducheneaut and Bellotti 2001; Whittaker and Sidner 1996).

We have already discussed one critical aspect of email management: ensuring that actionable items are dealt with to meet specific commitments. Consistent with design suggestions from Whittaker and Sidner (1996), some sophisticated modern email clients now allow users to configure their inbox to "snooze" actionable emails, making actionable items disappear from the inbox until their deadline arrives, when they reappear as inbox items (see, e.g., http://www.boomeranggmail.com/ or Inbox by Gmail). This snooze function has the benefit of reducing the number of distracter emails in the inbox, allowing users to focus on more critical items until their deadline arrives.

In spite of the central role of email in everyday work, we know relatively little about how people actually retrieve information from email. One exception is a study by Elsweiler, Baillie, and Ruthven (2008), who looked at people's ability to remember email messages. Participants were usually able to remember whether a message was in their email archive, and memory for specific information about each message was generally good, with users often able to remember multiple message attributes. People remembered content, purpose, or task-related information best, correctly recalling over 80 percent of this type of information—even when messages were months old. People were less good at remembering sender information; this type of information tended to be forgotten rather quickly. Memory for temporal information was worst of all, dropping to around 50 percent correct over several months. In all cases, memory was affected by both the age and size of the email archive, with users remembering less when they had bigger archives or when they were required to remember older items.

Dumais and colleagues (2003) also examined email access, and developed a new type of system, called *Stuff I've Seen* (SIS). SIS is a cross-format search engine allowing users to access files, email messages, and web pages by issuing a query in a single, unified interface. SIS also supports sorting of results via attributes such as date or author. In a large-scale deployment of SIS, Dumais et al. found that the majority of searches (74 percent) was focused on email as opposed to files. When searching for email messages, there was a very strong focus on recent items, with 21 percent of searched-for items being from the last week and almost 50 percent from the last month. Many of these searches (25 percent) included the name of the email sender in the query, suggesting (contrary to Elsweiler, Baillie, and Ruthven

2008) that sender name is a useful retrieval cue for email messages. In chapter 12 we describe the novel ContactMap email client, which exploits the salience of a sender name and provides social context for email data (Whittaker et al. 2004). How can we explain the prevalence of name-based search observed by Dumais and colleagues, compared to Elsweiler, Baillie, and Ruthven's (2008) results? Part of the difference may be due to the Dumais group's observations of naturalistic behaviors, which tended to be focused around retrieving recent email messages. In contrast, the Elsweiler team looked at longer-term access for more structured, lab-based tasks. In addition, Dumais and colleagues did not look at the success of searches; it may be that although sender information was used frequently in searches, these sender searches were often unsuccessful.

The most systematic naturalistic study of email refinding is by Whittaker et al. (2011). We compared the efficiency and success of two different types of retrieval strategies: (a) *preparatory* retrieval, which exploits subjectively organized folders created to anticipate the retrieval context; and (b) *opportunistic* approaches, which are not dependent on these prior organizational structures but instead rely on behaviors such as scrolling, sorting, or searching to retrieve information. There are clear trade-offs between these strategies; folders create a subjectively organized structure that can promote retrieval, but preparation requires effort that may not pay off—for example, if folders do not match retrieval requirements. To compare these different refinding strategies, we carried out a field study of 345 long-term users to explore the nature of email retrieval. We examined over eighty-five thousand refinding actions in a modern email client that supports search, folders, and conversational threading.

We recorded various refinding behaviors. We logged each instance of the following operations, along with its duration:

Folder access: Whenever users opened a folder.

Sort: Whenever users clicked various email header fields, such as sender, subject, date, time, attachments, and so on.

Scroll: Whenever users scrolled for more than one second (a conservative criterion adopted to identify when scrolling is used for refinding). This duration was based on pilot data that observed different scrolling actions.

Search: Whenever users conducted a search.

Each finding operation was treated separately, so opening a folder followed by a sort was treated as two separate operations, for example. We also recorded the success and duration of finding sequences; we define a *finding sequence* as a set of the previously listed refinding behaviors containing one or more sort, scroll, search, or folder-access operation. Our analysis was quantitative and relied on parsing large numbers of logfiles, so we employed an automatically implementable definition of success. We defined retrieval *success* as occurring whenever a user opened a target message and either (a) replied to it or (b) read the message for an extended period of time. Again, this threshold for extended reading was determined following pilots to evaluate how long it took users to read representative email messages.

We found that opportunistic retrieval strategies were more prevalent than preparatory foldering strategies, with folders being used for just 13 percent of overall accesses. By far, the most common strategy used to retrieve emails was to scroll through the inbox, which accounts for 62 percent of all retrieval actions. Both searches (18 percent of retrieval actions) and sorts

(6 percent) were also used, and these actions correlated with scrolling. This suggests that searches, sorts, and scrolling co-occur as part of a common finding sequence; that is, for example, someone might search for an email and then sort the results that the search generated, or someone might sort his or her inbox to look for a specific property (e.g., messages with attachments) and then scroll through those messages. However, we also found that high filers—people who had a higher proportion of their email in folders—were more likely to access information using those folders. They used those folders for accessing messages 16 percent of the time, compared to 7 percent for those who had lower proportions in folders. In contrast, low filers—people who had less information in folders—tended to rely on other retrieval strategies, such as search, scrolling, and sorting.

We then explored the overall efficiency and success of the preparatory foldering strategy. It takes time and effort to manually organize emails into folders, but does this effort pay off? Do people who prepare find information more quickly and successfully? Do they find information in fewer operations? These results are shown in table 4.1. As expected, we found that high filers (who had a higher proportion of emails in folders) found target messages while using fewer operations in each finding sequence. However, this did not equate to faster overall finding sequences, because high filers took marginally longer in their finding sequences. There is a simple explanation for this: high filers are more reliant on folder accesses, which take much longer than the searches and sorts. More important is how often people successfully find the target message. To control for the fact that people had different numbers of finding sequences, we evaluated what percentage of their finding sequences were

Table 4.1
Success and efficiency of finding sequences for high and low filers based on median split of percent messages in folders. High filers use fewer retrieval operations but take longer and are no more successful than low filers.

Measure	% Mailbox foldered	Mean	SD	Significance
% of all sequences that are successful	High	0.88	.12	$t(356) = 0.98$, $p > 0.05$
	Low	0.88	.11	
Sequence duration (secs)	High	72.87	38.05	$t(356) = 1.97$, $p < 0.05^*$
	Low	66.07	26.64	
# of operations	High	3.69	1.46	$t(356) = 2.17$, $p < 0.05^*$
	Low	4.16	2.50	

successful. We expected high filers to be more successful, given their investment in preparing materials for retrieval ("I know where that message is because I deliberately filed it"). Contrary to our expectations, high filers were no more successful at finding messages than low filers.

These are important findings. They show that although people who create complex folders indeed rely on these structures for retrieval, such preparatory behaviors are less efficient than opportunistic methods and do not improve retrieval success. In contrast, opportunistic behaviors such as search, scanning, and sorting promote faster and equally successful retrieval.

Accessing Photos

In chapter 3, we described how people organize their digital pictures and the rudimentary management strategies they employ. As with email research, there has been more focus on photo management and less examination of exploitation and the implications of different management schemes for access. Digital photos are a highly valued resource (Petrelli, Whittaker, and Brockmeier 2008; Whittaker, Bergman, and Clough 2010), so we should expect people to create effective ways to access them. Indeed, work on accessing recently taken photos shows that people are good at retrieving these (Frohlich et al. 2002). When Kirk and colleagues (2006) asked people to sort recent pictures in preparation for sharing them with friends or family, they found that participants were effective in finding and organizing pictures taken within the last year.

These findings contrast with our own work on parents' ability to retrieve older family pictures that were taken more than a year ago. Although these older pictures were judged as being highly valuable, participants were often unsuccessful in accessing them. In a variant of the EPIR procedure, we asked participants to name significant family events from more than a year ago that they had photographed digitally. In a subsequent retrieval task, participants were asked to show the interviewer digital pictures from three to five of these salient past events. To prevent participants from choosing events that they could retrieve easily, they were not told about the retrieval task during the initial interview. The interviewer asked participants to sit at their computers and show him pictures relating to these key events.

In contrast to their expectations, our participants were successful in retrieving pictures in only slightly more than half of the retrieval tasks (61 percent). In the remainder (39 percent), participants simply could not find pictures of these significant family events. Of the unsuccessful retrieval tasks, 75 percent involved pictures that the participants believed to be stored on their computer (or on CDs) but which they subsequently could not find. The remaining 25 percent were pictures participants initially thought were stored digitally, but during the retrieval process they changed their minds, thinking instead that the pictures had been taken with an analog camera.

Based on participants' comments and behavior during and after search, we identified several potential reasons for their unexpectedly poor retrieval performance: keeping too many pictures, distributed storage across multiple devices leading to misidentifying where they had stored a picture, unsystematic organization, false familiarity, and lack of maintenance. In our discussion of keeping and management in chapters 2 and 3, we noted the tendency to overkeep pictures and a lack of systematic organization; we now explore the implications of these behaviors for retrieval.

The most frequent explanation participants gave for their difficulties in retrieving pictures was of the sheer volume of pictures they had to access. Consistent with previous findings (Frohlich et al. 2002; Kirk et al. 2006; Rodden and Wood 2003), participants felt that they were taking many more pictures with digital cameras than they had with analog equipment. All participants explained such overkeeping by pointing to the low cost of capturing large numbers of digital pictures. However, it was only during retrieval that they realized so many pictures made it hard for them to locate a target from the thousands they had retained.

Some participants attempted to explain their poor retrieval by arguing that they had not given folders meaningful names. Although 67 percent of participants made efforts to apply labels, such labeling did not seem to guarantee retrieval, possibly because people's naming schemes were inconsistent.

Furthermore, people who used meaningful labels were neither more successful nor faster at retrieving pictures. Participants' comments and behaviors also suggested that the meaning of these labels had been forgotten over time. Finally, participants commented on difficulties in remembering long-term changes in organizational schemes they had adopted or software they had used.

The lack of organization in people's collections meant that they were overreliant on trial and error strategies for accessing their photos. Consistent with studies of autobiographical memory (Brewer 1988; Wagenaar 1986), some of our participants tried to use knowledge of related events as temporal landmarks to estimate the approximate date on which the target event occurred. They then navigated using that landmark date to the folder they thought might contain the target pictures. Specific folders were chosen because their names (if there were meaningful names) were thought to relate to the target or because a folder date was close to the estimated date.

Others tried to remember the exact date when the event had occurred and to locate folders from that date. Participants who consistently created time-based folder names (e.g., Spring13) were more successful than those using other naming schemes, although only a minority of participants used this strategy. However, there are problems with relying exclusively on system-generated temporal information. First, as we have seen, participants are often unable to accurately remember the date of the target event. Second, the system-generated date label may be inaccurate, either because of problems with camera settings or because the folder date represents the upload date as opposed to when the picture was actually taken.

Overall, retrieval strategies most often seemed to involve trial and error: users would cycle through their entire photo collection, accessing folders to see whether they contained promising pictures and moving on to other folders if they did not.

Accessing Web Pages

The problems of accessing web pages have been much studied. We have already observed that most people's intuitions about web access are incorrect; they believe that people typically rely on search to access web information. A second incorrect intuition is that web accesses follow the pattern of information foraging—in other words, that people predominantly seek out new information from the web.

In reality, however, it turns out that search is less frequent than we might expect. In addition, users focus on refinding rather than seeking novel information. Instead of foraging for new information, users tend to reaccess previously visited data using a variety of simple browser techniques, including following links, retyping URLs, or using the back button (Aula, Jhaveri, and Kaki 2005; Bruce, Jones, and Dumais 2004; Obendorf et al. 2007).

One possible reason for this belief in the dominance of search is that historically web users moved from relying on navigation that exploited human-generated categories to using search tools. Early web tools such as Yahoo! provided human-generated taxonomies of what were then relatively small collections of web documents. Users accessed pages by browsing through these links. However, one obvious limitation of these manual taxonomic techniques is that they are completely infeasible for the billions of documents that are now on the web.

Many studies analyze logfiles and history lists to measure exactly how users locate information on the web, documenting the extent to which web accesses involve seeking novel information versus refinding. Early work looking at students' web access behaviors showed a characteristic pattern: hub-and-spoke accesses. In this pattern, users find a useful, authoritative resource—a hub. They then fan out to the various links (spokes) from this resource hub, usually traversing no more than two links before reaccessing the hub using the back button (Catledge and Pitkow 1995). Tauscher and Greenberg (1997) instrumented browsers and looked at the rate at which people returned to previously visited sites. They documented a recurrence rate of 58 percent, finding also that the majority of each individual user's overall accesses involved a small set of websites that the user frequently reaccessed. Revisits are prevalent, as indicated by the use of the back button, which accounts for around 30 percent of all web actions. In addition, Tauscher and Greenberg found that people were much more likely to reaccess sites that they had visited recently. Cockburn and Greenberg (2000) carried out a similar study, finding that a much higher proportion of accesses (81 percent) were revisits.

Another study, conducted by Wen (2003), was unusual in that it looked at the *success* of refinding. He asked users to conduct typical web access sessions and then to retrieve information that they had found useful in the search sessions. Users were able to successfully reaccess only 20 percent of the sites they had visited. Finally, and consistent with other results (Teevan et al. 2004), Wen (2003) found that the general strategy for reaccess was to try to retrace prior actions rather than attempting to search or to type in prior URLs.

Aula, Jhaveri, and Kaki (2005) looked at users' self-reported strategies for web search and reaccess. They found that having multiple windows or tabs open was very common because reaccess was prevalent. In addition, the most commonly reported ways to reaccess information were to reaccess links, search for information again, directly type a URL, or save pages as local files. This confirms the results of an observational study by Bruce, Jones, and Dumais (2004), which documented that the most prevalent strategy for refinding was to type in a URL directly. Other access strategies were much less prevalent—for example, emailing links to oneself, adding URLs to a website, or writing down queries. Finally, although history lists provide an intuitive way to reaccess information, they are used strikingly infrequently. Aula, Jhaveri, and Kaki (2005) found various problems with history lists: Not only are web page titles often misleading, but the list also intermingles successful and unsuccessful results—making it hard for users to focus on valuable information. Both Aula and colleagues and Wen (2003) also noted user problems with reaccessing web information; in particular, using prior search queries to refind information is difficult, because successful search is an iterative process that often involves multiple queries. During initial retrieval, users may have tried multiple strategies to find information, exploring sites that later turned out to be dead ends. While later trying to reaccess a target site, users were often unable to distinguish successful prior searches from these failed searches. This made it hard for users to regenerate successful queries. Users also often could not recall the exact method that they used for access, and as a result they could be unable to reconstruct a search query for information for which they had originally browsed.

In perhaps the best controlled study of web access, Obendorf and colleagues (2007) preprocessed sets of URLs for twenty-five users and found that revisiting rates in prior studies might have been artificially inflated by sites that automatically refreshed without user intervention. When they controlled for such automatic refreshes, revisitation levels were around 41 percent. They also documented a variety of general strategies used to access pages. The most common were using a hyperlink (44 percent of accesses), using forms—including the use of search engines (15 percent), using the back button (14 percent), opening a new tab or window (11 percent), and typing in the URL directly (9 percent).

Turning specifically to revisits (as opposed to all retrievals), Obendorf and colleagues (2007) again found that the most common strategy for refinding information was to follow links (50 percent), with the back button being the next most common strategy (31 percent). The remaining direct access strategies (using bookmarks, homepage links, history, or direct entry of URLs) accounted for the final 13 percent of accesses. As in previous studies, reaccesses tended to be for recently visited sites; 73 percent of revisits occur within an hour of the first visit, which makes the reported use of the back button appear rather low. One possible reason for the relatively low numbers of back accesses may be that the tabbing facilities provided by new browsers mean that users are not as reliant on hub-and-spoke types of reaccesses. They can therefore retain the context of their hub page while using tabs to manage follow-up spoke pages.

Finally, Obendorf and colleagues (2007) looked at how access strategies varied as a function of the length of time since the original page access. Again, there were huge recency effects: 50

percent of revisits occurred within three minutes, and the dominant strategy here was to use the back button, presumably because the target information was readily available in the browser cache. For revisits occurring within an hour, the back button and links were the most common ways to refind data. Between an hour and a day, back button usage decreased hugely, with users becoming more reliant on links and direct access (typing in the URL). Between a day and a week, links and typing URLs were the most common strategies, and at intervals of greater than a week, use of links dominated. This greater reliance on links may reflect an orienteering strategy (Teevan et al. 2004), in which users gradually home in on target information, typically by searching for it first and then using links to focus on the exact information. In any case, the results clearly show that access strategies are quite varied and are heavily dependent on the time interval between initial access and reaccess. Part of the reason for this is technical; for very short term reaccesses, information is directly available in the cache, whereas at longer intervals this is unlikely to be true. In addition, cognitive factors may be at work here. At medium and longer reaccess intervals, users may have created multiple windows or tabs and may be unable to remember which of these they first used to access the data.

Finally, the majority of revisits (73 percent) occur within an hour, 12 percent between an hour and a day, 9 percent between a day and a week, and 8 percent at longer intervals. As we have seen, the time between accesses is a critical factor influencing retrieval, and because the majority of revisits occurs in the short term, certain strategies (such as using the back button or link-based access) are prevalent overall.

To summarize, web retrieval often involves reaccessing previously visited pages. Use of links, tabs, and the back button is prevalent for more recently accessed pages. Search tends not to occur very often. Users also tend to access a small number of sites.

Summary

During exploitation, people's preference is for manual methods (folder navigation/following links), whether this is for regular files or web data. Search is a less preferred option, even for web documents. We present extensive evidence for this navigation preference in chapter 5, in which we directly compare retrieval methods for personal files. Search is infrequent with personal photos; content-based techniques are weak, and there is very little metadata. As a result, people have to rely on browsing, which turns out to be ineffective for older data in many cases.

Email messages are different from files: Search can be useful for informative items, because people are able to remember certain information about messages (names/content), at least in the short term. However, reminding is needed for actionable items, and search cannot be used, because searching is a deliberate act that implies the user has already remembered the action related to the item. Users therefore have to rely on scanning their inboxes for actionable items, which is often inefficient because of the amount of heterogeneous information that inboxes currently contain.

Contradicting people's intuitions, search is not the prevalent way to access web data. Reaccesses are common, with people using the back button or hyperlinks as their main reaccess methods. Reaccesses usually return to recently accessed information, and the exact reaccess strategy depends on how recently the target item was last accessed.

Mismatches sometimes occur between retrieval structures and their exploitation. For photos, there seems to be a failure to create retrieval-appropriate structures, which occurs in part because these structures are not frequently accessed; as a result, retrieval is often unsuccessful for older materials. For email messages, some people spend large amounts of time creating folder structures that may not be efficient to exploit. For web documents, people often create structures (such as bookmark collections) that are not used because there are less costly ways to access information.

Exploitation has clear regularities; there is a strong bias toward access of recent items, and a bias toward accessing a small number of items very frequently. Retrieval techniques such as recent document lists capitalize on this tendency.

Part I: Summary

We began by arguing that prevailing intuitions about information behaviors are inaccurate (chapter 1). People are not exclusively consumers of new public information. Instead, their information behaviors often involve curation, in which they keep and manage valued personal information for future access. Curation can be viewed as a form of *self-directed communication* in which a user keeps and organizes personal information using subjective attributes that can be understood by the user's future self.

Those observations led us to outline a three-stage model of curation, and we characterized the key curation processes of keeping, management, and exploitation (chapters 2–4). In general, users tend to overkeep information, with the exception of valued contacts and web pages. With respect to managing information, we reviewed evidence suggesting some benefits for piles as well as files, although organizing actionable information remains a major challenge. Exploitation remains reliant on manual methods such as navigation, in spite of the emergence of desktop search. Both keeping and management decisions are demanding, because they require users to predict the future—in particular, what information their future selves will need, as well as how they will be thinking about their information in the future.

Curation problems are becoming more pressing as people's personal archives continue to grow. It has been argued that current technologies are obsolete and inadequate to address these problems. In particular, folders are said to be outdated and to suffer significant technical limitations. Several new technologies have been proposed to replace them, and we turn to these in part II of the book. There, we review our own studies evaluating preferences for folder-based navigation versus search and evaluations of new technologies, such as tagging and cloud-based group information management. In each case, our work shows that there is little empirical support for replacing subjectively organized folders with these newer technologies, and the last chapter of part II (chapter 8) provides cognitive and neurological reasons for this preference for folder-based organization and retrieval.

II Hierarchical Folders and Their Alternatives

Despite a continuous stream of proposed new technologies to support PIM, folders remain the main way in which people manage and retrieve their personal information. In this part of the book, we describe the characteristics of folders and outline common arguments about their potential limitations.

When using folders, people first find or create a folder that characterizes an information item. They later retrieve the item from that folder by manually navigating to it. The term *folders* originates from paper folders, which are physical containers that hold together different paper documents belonging to the same category. The overall category name may be written on the back of the folder. Paper folders usually contain paper documents, and similarly, virtual folders usually contain virtual files. Virtual folders also have names to describe their content. Unlike paper folders, virtual folders can also contain subfolders, which in turn can hold files and sub-subfolders and so on. This is called a folder hierarchy.

Folders descended from directories. The first operating system to enable personal storage by exploiting hierarchical directories was developed in the mid-1960s and was called *Multics*. In Multics, users were allocated personal directories in which they could create their own subdirectories, sub-subdirectories, and so on, and they could store their files in any of these "locations." This directory structure was later applied to the Unix and Linux operating systems. The location metaphor became even clearer with the creation of digital folders, introduced in the Xerox Star in 1981. A virtual folder is a visual metaphor for a location: Users can see information items "inside" folders and can manipulate items and folders in various straightforward ways—for example, dragging and dropping information items from one folder to another. Of course, these directories and folders do not really contain information items from a computer science point of view, but they appear to do so from the user's perspective. Thus, for the sake of simplicity, we refer to them in this manner. This folder hierarchy metaphor was later applied by Apple to the Mac operating systems and then by Microsoft to the Windows operating system. Thus, location-based storage has been used without significant modifications, continuously, and almost exclusively for several decades.

Throughout most of its long history, the hierarchical method has met with criticism. One disadvantage is that classification of information can hide it from the user. Putting a file inside a folder reduces the chances of visual reminding—an important task for actionable information, as described in chapter 3 (Malone 1983; Kidd 1994; Whittaker and Sidner 1996). The act of categorizing may also prove to be cognitively challenging, because information items don't fit into folders neatly (Dumais et al. 2003). Most importantly, Lansdale (1988) argued that by imitating storage in the physical world, hierarchical folders wrongly force users to store a file in a single location when it may belong in several categories. This in turn forces users to remember the exact location of an information item at the time of retrieval. Remembering this location can be difficult, especially when a long time has passed between storage and retrieval.

These apparent problems with folders and navigation caused PIM researchers to turn to alternative solutions designed to overcome such perceived limitations. Three major proposed alternatives are search, tags, and group classification, all of which we touched on in part I. *Search* allows users to potentially retrieve an information item in one shot using any attribute they happen to remember about the information item and is therefore more flexible and efficient than navigation. *Tags* allow users to apply multiple categorizations to the same information item, thus avoiding having to classify and retrieve information using a single attribute. Group information management avoids the duplication of shared files and their organization and allows users to devolve some of the work of organization to others.

The first three chapters of part II compare the hierarchical, folder-based method to these three alternatives. The focus of these chapters is on management and retrieval of personal files. Each chapter is based on large-scale, multimethod studies we have conducted. These chapters show that when given the choice, participants prefer folders over these alternate technologies. This gives rise to a paradox: Why do users persist in using folders when they seem to have multiple intuitive limitations? We provide answers in chapter 8, which offers a *cognitive explanation* for navigation preferences. We report two different studies that show people prefer folders and navigation because they place fewer demands on cognitive resources—in particular, on verbal attention that many psychological studies have shown to be limited in its capacity. These two studies use convergent methods; the first uses traditional cognitive psychology approaches, and the second uses neuroscientific methods.

5 The Search Alternative

This chapter discusses how we retrieve our personal files—that is, the exploitation process. We will focus on two main ways of retrieving personal information, navigation and search, in order to determine which one is the preferred retrieval method of users. To quickly recap, *navigation* is a two-phase process: First, users manually traverse their organizational hierarchies until they reach the folder where the target item is stored. Second, they locate the target within that folder by visually scanning the folder's contents. *Search* is a process in which users first generate a query specifying one or more attributes of the target item—for example, its name (or part of it), text it contains, its modification date, and so forth. The desktop search engine then returns a set of results, from which the user selects the sought-for item.

A commonly held view is that search is a simpler and more efficient process than navigation (Russell and Lawrence 2007; Cutrell, Dumais, and Teevan 2006) and that search is replacing navigation as a method of finding files. This chapter is based on research we conducted that evaluated this *search everything* assumption—that is, the idea that improvements in search technology mean that search will replace navigation as the main way of accessing personal information and eliminate the need for organization within folders (Bergman et al. 2008).

The Search Everything Approach

There are obvious intuitive advantages of search for both retrieval and organization: Search seems to be more flexible and efficient for retrieval. It is flexible because it does not depend on users remembering the correct storage location; instead, users can specify any file attribute they happen to remember in their queries (Lansdale 1988). Search is also potentially more efficient, because users can retrieve information by generating a single query instead of using multiple operations to laboriously navigate to the relevant part of the folder hierarchy. Finally, search doesn't require careful organizational preparation. Researchers claim that search finesses the management problem; users don't have to engage in complex organizational strategies that exhaustively anticipate their future retrieval requirements (Cutrell, Dumais, and Teevan 2006; Lansdale 1988; Russell and Lawrence 2007; Dourish et al. 2000). These arguments against navigation are bolstered by developments in web access. As we saw in chapter 4, use of navigational systems such as Yahoo! categories to retrieve web data has largely been replaced by other methods (Kobayashi and Takeda 2000; Obendorf et al. 2007).

These intuitive arguments have led many PIM researchers to propose that search engines should replace folders. For example, when presenting their new operating system prototype, Placeless Documents, Dourish and colleagues wrote the following:

Unfortunately, strict hierarchical structures can map poorly to user needs ... while strict hierarchies of locations may provide a logical structure for document storage (meeting the needs of the system), they provide less useful support for document interaction (failing to meet the needs of users) ... Our approach is based on document properties, rather than document locations. Properties are the primary, uniform means for organizing, grouping, managing, controlling, and retrieving documents. Document properties are features of a document that are meaningful to users, rather than to the system. Documents can have any number of properties, reflecting the different features that might be relevant to users at different times or in different contexts. (Dourish et al. 2000, 141–142)

Similar ideas about the limits of hierarchical organization and the contrasting benefits of search are presented in publications with titles such as *Searching to Eliminate Personal Information Management* (Cutrell, Dumais, and Teevan 2006) and *Search Everything* (Russell and Lawrence 2007), as well as other publications that propose radical new alternatives to folder-based navigation (Fertig, Freeman, and Gelernter 1996a; Raskin 2000; Lansdale 1988). For simplicity, we will call these views the *search everything* approach.

The focus on search-based retrieval has led to the development of several experimental PIM search engines, such as Phlat (Cutrell et al. 2006), SIS (Dumais et al. 2003), Haystack (Adar, Karger, and Stein 1999), and Raton Laveur (Bellotti and Smith 2000), as well as commercial systems such as Einfish Personal, Copernic Desktop Search, Yahoo! Desktop Search, and Microsoft Desktop Search. Although these systems argue for the superiority of search, they nevertheless do not completely reject hierarchical folders, instead proposing a hybrid approach in which files can be retrieved by either search or navigation. Other systems take a more radical approach to retrieving personal information by completely eliminating folder-based storage. Such systems include Lifestreams (Freeman and Gelernter 1996b), Canon Cat (Raskin 2000), Presto (Dourish et al. 1999), Placeless Documents (Dourish et al. 2000), MyLifeBits (Gemmell et al. 2002), and iMeMex (Blunschi et al. 2007).

To sum up, the search everything approach makes the following claims about the benefits of search for both file retrieval and organization: Regarding retrieval, it claims that search is more efficient and flexible and therefore maps better to user requirements. Regarding management, users are known to have problems organizing files effectively for retrieval (Dumais et al. 2003; Whittaker and Sidner 1996); the claim here is that search eliminates the need for such organization. These proposed benefits naturally lead to a prediction: If search meets user requirements so well, then users should prefer it over navigation. The next section reports early studies exploring this preference for navigation versus search.

Early Evidence Regarding User Preferences

Evidence concerning users' search preferences comes from empirical studies that examine retrieval behavior. An early paper concerning users' retrieval habits (Barreau and Nardi 1995) combined Barreau's interviews of novice personal computer users (using DOS, Windows 3.1, and OS/2) with Nardi's interviews of experienced Mac users. In both cases, users "overwhelmingly" preferred to navigate to their files rather than to search for them. Similar preferences for navigation were observed in more recent studies (Boardman and Sasse 2004; Capra and Pérez-Quiñones 2005; Kirk et al. 2006; Teevan et al. 2004). Regarding management, in another qualitative study

(Jones, Phuwanartnurak, et al. 2005), thirteen out of fourteen participants replied negatively to the following hypothetical question: "Suppose you could find your personal information using a simple search rather than your current folders. Can we take your folders away?"

These early findings raise a question: If search better suits user requirements, then why do people prefer navigation? One argument is that search technology is still immature. For example, Fertig, Freeman, and Gelernter (1996a) argued that these navigation preferences result from limitations in search technology and that improvements in search would inevitably lead to the replacement of navigation. Fertig and colleagues noted that the PIM search engines at that time (the mid-1990s) were "slow, difficult, or only operate[d] on file names (not content)" and did not provide incremental indexing. They further speculated that "inclusion of these better search techniques into current systems could sway results" (67).

The Big Leap in Desktop Search Engines

We can happily report that all the improvements that Fertig, Freeman, and Gelernter (1996a) anticipated are now incorporated into commercial desktop search engines. The big leap in search engine technology resulted from an important technical innovation in indexing. Advanced search engines (such as Google Desktop and Apple's Spotlight) now generate a real-time index that is constantly updated, as opposed to older search engines (such as Windows XP Search Companion and Apple's Sherlock) that incrementally accessed actual files scattered across the users' hard disk. As a result, improved search engines are one thousand times faster than old ones when tested on the same computers (Farina 2005; Lowe 2006). The fact that retrieval time has decreased from minutes to fractions of a second allows for the following important improvements to search engines:

User-centered design: In older search engines, users had to choose between either file name search or full text search (i.e., searching the contents of files). They also had to decide whether they wanted to specify the time at which the target file had recently been modified. To achieve a reasonable retrieval time, users needed to input more information to allow the computer to do less, an approach that reflects a machine-oriented design. Improved search engines are more user-centric; their increased retrieval speed allows them to reduce query definition steps and complications. This promotes greater choice and flexibility in defining queries.

Incremental search: Another advantage of advanced search engines is that they support incremental search, so the search begins as soon as the user types the first character of the query. This has the benefit of being interactive, allowing users to refine their query in light of the results returned and halt the query after typing just a few characters if the target item is already in view. Older search engines were less efficient, prompting the user via form filling to specify multiple attribute fields and press Enter before the query would be sent. Incrementality, according to Raskin (2000), has several advantages: (a) the user and computer do not have to wait for each other; (b) users know when they have typed enough to disambiguate their queries, because the desired file appears in the display; and (c) users receive constant feedback as to the results of the search—allowing them to correct spelling mistakes or refine search words without interrupting their search.

Cross-format search: Another limitation of older-generation search engines was that users could only search one file format at a time. Following the SIS (Dumais et al. 2003) initiative, current-generation search engines support search across multiple datatypes; files, emails, instant messages, and web history are retrieved from the same search query. Cross-format search allows improved search engines to address the project fragmentation problem in which information items related to the same project but in different formats are stored in different locations. For example, documents and emails about the same project may appear in different parts of the file system (Bergman, Beyth-Marom, and Nachmias 2006). We discuss this further in chapter 11 where we expand on the project fragmentation problem and present our own solution to address it.

Given these improvements in desktop search engines, we felt that it was time to revisit the search everything hypothesis. If the availability of improved desktop search engines leads to a substantial increase in search, then it is reasonable to assume that this effect will continue as search engines improve. If, on the other hand, no such increase in search is found, it raises questions regarding claims that improved search engines affect retrieval preferences and file organization. Our study (Bergman et al. 2008) focused on files, because they are considered by most users to be central to their personal information collections (Bergman 2006; Boardman 2004).

Evaluation of the Search Everything Approach

The search everything approach is based on deeply rooted intuitions among researchers, so evaluating it required a thorough evaluation of different operating systems and search engines. We wanted to avoid our results being specific to a single search engine and research method. To achieve this, we used a multi-method research design: We tested the same research questions using different search engines and different research methods by conducting two complementary studies, one longitudinal and one cross-sectional.

Specifically, we conducted two studies addressing the same research questions and using variants of the same questionnaire, but testing different search engines and using different research methods:

Windows study: The Windows study was a longitudinal study in which we installed the Google Desktop search engine on the personal computers of forty-seven Windows XP users who had used the Windows Search Companion search engine. We wanted to explore the effect of an intervention in which we trained participants about the functions of a search engine and encouraged them to use it. We wanted to see whether experience with search would change their retrieval preferences. We used a within-subjects research design—a method in which each of the participants experiences more than one condition with their behaviors in these different conditions being compared. We compared the frequency of search use before and after we trained a set of participants to use search, and we administered a questionnaire regarding retrieval habits before installing Google Desktop. Participants completed the questionnaire twice more: after three weeks during which they had been asked to use Google Desktop instead of navigating to their files, and then again seven months later. This process allowed us to test the longitudinal effect on participants' retrieval habits.

Mac study: In the Mac study, we explored the effects of search engine quality on retrieval by comparing the retrieval preferences of 519 Mac OS X 10.4 users who used the more advanced Spotlight search engine with those of seventy Mac OS 10.0–10.3 users who used the older Sherlock search engine. Each set of participants used a different search engine throughout, making this a between-subjects design (a research design method that compares the behaviors of two or more different groups of participants). Because of the between-subjects design, participants could not guess the aim of the study and bias it.

We administered the same questionnaire in both studies. In the questionnaire, participants were asked to estimate the frequency with which they used each of the retrieval options (search, navigation, recent documents, and desktop shortcuts, with the addition of Smart Folders for Macs), expressed as a percentage of their total file retrievals. Two measures were extracted from their responses: estimated search percentage and estimated navigation percentage.

Our research clearly relied on participants' ability to accurately estimate their retrieval preferences. To validate these estimates, we compared them with actual retrieval behaviors in two independent prestudies. Both studies showed extremely high correlations between estimates and actual retrieval behavior (with the search percentage being slightly overestimated), indicating that users' estimates of their search percentages are accurate and valid.

Our overall results suggest that adherents of the search everything approach to PIM may be mistaken in their claims about both retrieval and storage. Regarding retrieval, more than a decade after Fertig, Freeman, and Gelernter (1996a) predicted that the availability of improved search engines would increase the preference for search over navigation, our results indicated that they do not. Regarding storage, two decades after Lansdale (1988) suggested search as an alternative to the hierarchical method, our results showed that improved search engines do not lead to reduced reliance on folders.

We found a strong overall preference for navigation. Users estimated that they used navigation for a majority of their retrievals (between 56 percent and 68 percent). The average estimated search percentages were much lower: 11 to 15 percent for Google Desktop, Sherlock, and Spotlight users and 7 percent for Windows Search Companion users (possibly because the search option was less visible with that search engine). These results confirm the navigation preference originally observed by Barreau and Nardi (1995) and more recently by others (Boardman and Sasse 2004; Capra and Pérez-Quiñones 2005; Kirk et al. 2006; Teevan et al. 2004). In addition, the evaluated search percentage seems to be quite stable and unaffected by a user's age, years of computer use, evaluated experience, and hours of daily use. A later study (Blau, Madmon, and Bergman 2013) also found that the estimated search percentage is unaffected by computer literacy. In other words, computer experts are no more likely to use search than novices.

To summarize, in two different research designs for Windows and Mac, we tested our main research question: Do improved search engines induce more search, both in absolute terms and also relative to navigation? In the Windows study, the installation of Google Desktop significantly increased the estimated search percentage of Windows Search Companion users from 7 percent to 15 percent on average after three weeks of use. However, seven months later, the estimated search percentage dropped back to 10 percent, which was not significantly higher than the original baseline. The Mac study, which had a larger number of participants (589), found no increase in search at all when using an improved search engine. Altogether, the results show a limited and inconsistent effect of improved search engines on retrieval preferences. Therefore, our results indicate that improved search engines do not affect the preference for navigation over search.

These results are consistent with actual retrieval behaviors found in log studies, which also show low search usage. In studies deploying two experimental search engines—Stuff I've Seen (SIS; Dumais et al. 2003) and Phlat (Cutrell et al. 2006)—results reported an average of a single file retrieval every two days and once a week, respectively. Because the participants (who were Microsoft employees) were likely to be retrieving many files each day, it would be safe to conclude that neither search engine led to a preference for search over navigation or to a dramatic increase in search. Another more recent log study, which tracked absolute percentages of search as a function of all file retrievals, also confirms that search is not preferred (Fitchett and Cockburn 2015). Mac users with a more advanced version of Spotlight than our own study used search for only 4 percent of all retrievals. This result is also consistent with our prestudies, which indicated that participants tend to overestimate their search percentage.

Why, then, is search so infrequent? A possible reason is that search is only used when people forget a file location. Our own results confirm Barreau and Nardi's (1995) observation that search was typically used as a last resort when users couldn't remember a file's location. Most users (between 73 percent and 82 percent across the different studies) spontaneously noted that they usually searched when they did not know where their files were located and estimated that the majority of their searches were performed when they had forgotten the file location (an average ranging between 83 percent and 97 percent for the different studies). According to participants' reports, only a tiny percentage of retrievals were searches for files for which locations were known (from none for Windows XP to an average of 4 percent for Google Desktop).

One way of thinking about this is that the percentage of files for which users don't remember their exact location might be regarded as an upper limit to search usage. This upper limit was estimated by our participants to be about 25 percent and was not affected by using an improved search engine or by a participant's age. For all conditions, we found that the average estimated search percentage is lower than the average estimated unknown locations percentage. This means that when participants didn't know the file location, they often still preferred not to search for it and instead to retrieve it in other ways. Therefore, a less ambitious—but perhaps more realistic—challenge for search engine developers could be to support search for the 25 percent of files for which users can't remember their locations.

In addition, the results show little support for the second major search everything hypothesis: that improvements in search engines lead to less reliance on hierarchical storage when organizing files. Only twelve of 481 Spotlight users reported that an improved search engine resulted in their being less organized or using fewer, more general, folders. Indeed, a different twelve participants reported that search led them to become *more* organized or to use deeper hierarchies with more subfolders. Furthermore, there was no significant difference in estimated unknown location percentage between improved and older search engines. Thus, there was no indication that the use of improved search engines led people to be more casual about how they organized information, inducing a poorer memory for where information was located. Altogether, these results confirm the results of Jones, Phuwanartnurak, et al. (2005), who showed that improved search engines do not reduce reliance on hierarchical storage.

Summary

Overall, our results show a preference for navigation over search regardless of the quality of the search engine people used. By no means does this imply that improving search engines is a waste of time. If search engines are indeed the PIM "fire escapes" to be used as a last resort, then in case of an emergency users obviously want to have the best escape route available. For those occasions in which users are frustrated because they forgot where they located their files, they should find accurate search engines to be of great importance. However, in light of our findings, there is still no evidence that what prevents users from using search as a preferred retrieval strategy is the "primitive" nature of current search engines: improving search engines did not change users' clear preference for navigation for personal information retrieval.

Following the arguments that Fertig, Freeman, and Gelernter made in 1996 (Fertig, Freeman, and Gelernter 1996a), one might still maintain that although search engines have greatly improved, they are still not sophisticated enough, and when *even more advanced* search engines are deployed, search will then be preferred to navigation. Although this remains a possibility, it has yet to be demonstrated. If our results had shown that improved search engines resulted in a substantial increase in search, it could be reasonably assumed that further improvements would eventually lead to the dominance of search. However, this was not found to be true. Instead, our study (Bergman et al. 2008) provides support for the view that in current PIM environments, there is an inherent preference for navigation, irrespective of a search engine's sophistication. In chapter 8, we will explore cognitive reasons for why this might be the case.

6   The Tagging Alternative

Like search, tagging is an alternative to folders that is frequently proposed in the PIM literature. It is widely claimed that tags have two fundamental advantages over folders: Tags enable multiple classification and eliminate the need for hierarchies. Let's explore these arguments in more detail:

Multiple classification: When using folders, an information item can only be stored in a single folder; however, users may be able to think of a number of possible classifications for that item (Dourish et al. 2000). For example, pictures from a conference in Copenhagen might be stored under Pictures, Trips, Conferences, or Copenhagen. One limitation of folders is that, as time passes, users may forget the single classification they made when first filing an item, making retrieval difficult or impossible. In contrast, tagging enables users to apply any number of tags to their information items and to use any of those tags to retrieve it. Applying more than a single tag to an information item is called *multiple classification.*

No hierarchical location: As we mentioned previously, folders may hide information items from view because they do not show items contained in subfolders (Malone 1983). The tagging approach consciously dispenses with hierarchies and locations. Instead, all information items are stored in a single, flat repository and are retrieved via nonhierarchical means, such as tag search, tag selection, or tag clouds.

Based on Bergman et al. (2013a), this chapter will examine tag versus folder preference to test the preceding two arguments.

Folders May Cause Unnatural Organization Behaviors

When presenting criticisms of folder hierarchies in the previous chapter, we deliberately skipped over the criticisms regarding single classification and folder location (presented briefly at the start of this chapter). Let's now examine these issues in detail.

Single Classification

Folder hierarchies typically enforce a single classification; however, in the user's mind, an information item often can fit into several different categories (Dourish et al. 2000). Therefore, when using folders, a user needs to decide which category fits best, a process that can be cognitively challenging (Lansdale 1988; Malone 1983; Dumais and Landauer 1983). As discussed in chapter 3, such categorization also needs to anticipate future usage (Bruce 2005), which may be difficult, because usage may change over time (Kidd 1994). This causes a retrieval problem, one that is clearly articulated by Lansdale (1988): "Placing a document into a filing system under one category places the information out of reach if retrieval is required for some other reason" (57). True, folder hierarchies do allow for shortcuts or aliases from one folder to another. However, this seems to go against the usual understanding of folder systems in which each folder represents a unique location where a file can reside

(Civan et al. 2008). Consequently, these other shortcut or alias options are rarely implemented by users in practice (Bergman 2006; Dourish et al. 2000). The limitation imposed by single classification in the hierarchical method is well documented in the PIM literature (Dourish et al. 2000; Lansdale 1988; Hsieh et al. 2008; Bloehdorn and Völkel 2006; Marsden and Cairns 2003; Quan et al. 2003; Heckner, Heilemann, and Wolff 2009).

The Hierarchical Locations Metaphor

Malone (1983) noted that filing (which in his study involved filing paper documents into physical folders) has a crucial disadvantage: filed documents lose their reminding function (i.e., ability to become aware of the information item without thinking about it). This may be a major problem for actionable information. As one of Malone's participants said, "You don't want to put it [a pile on the desk] away [inside a folder] because that way you'll never come across it again" (107). The notion that folders can "hide" files is repeatedly mentioned in PIM literature (Jones, Phuwanartnurak, et al. 2005; Lansdale 1988; Civan et al. 2008). Quan et al. (2003) complain that users must remember the ordered sequence of topics and subtopics that were used to organize information when attempting to retrieve it, even though the topics of interest during retrieval might be different than those during organization. Concerning emails, Elsweiler, Baillie, and Ruthven (2011) argue that users find retrieval more difficult when emails are organized in folders than when left in the inbox. This claim gets some support from the Whittaker et al. (2011) study of email refinding (chapter 4). In that study, we also found that emails organized in folders were not retrieved faster than those left in the inbox.

The Tag Everything Approach

The criticisms noted in the previous section motivate a model in which tags are proposed as an improvement over folders. We will call this model the *tag everything* approach. Tags are a kind of metadata that describe an information item through keywords or terms. Unlike folders, tags are nonhierarchical, and users can assign as many tags as they want to an information item. In other words, in contrast to folders, tags do not commit a user to remembering a single unique location and a label indicating where a file is stored. Additional psychological arguments for tags are suggested by Hsieh et al. (2008), who claim that tags are more compatible with human cognition than folders: "In contrast to the hierarchy model, Collins and Loftus have proposed a spreading activation model of semantic processing. The non-hierarchical structure of semantic processing is similar to that of flat-structure tag networks. ... Since most data stored in computers are declarative concepts, user-defined tags can be viewed as cognitive nodes in a concept network" (1–2). In recent years, there has been extensive development of tag-related PIM prototypes, including Phlat (Cutrell et al. 2006), TagFS (Bloehdorn and Völkel 2006), Gnowsis (Sauermann et al. 2006), ConTag (Adrian, Sauermann, and Roth-Berghofer 2007), TapGlance (Robbins 2008), Zotero (Ma and Wiedenbeck 2009), TAGtivity (Oleksik et al. 2009), BlueMail (Tang et al. 2008; Whittaker et al. 2011) and TagStore (Voit, Andrews, and Slany 2012).

Web 2.0
The Web 2.0 revolution, in which users share their content on the Internet, has had a crucial effect on the uptake of tag usage. Websites such as Flickr and YouTube allow users to upload their

pictures and videos to the Internet together with tags that describe this content. Via these tags, other users can search for this user-provided content. In a paper entitled "Why Do Tagging Systems Work?" Furnas et al. (2006) attribute the success of tagging to the social aspect of Web 2.0:

Tagging systems have become increasingly popular after an element of social interaction was introduced. Social Tagging Systems connect the individual bookmarking activities of users into a network of tags and resources shared among multiple users. Social tagging systems, then, allow users to share their tags for particular resources. The tag sharing allows multiple added benefits, in discovery as well as retrieval ... Social tagging systems may thus offer a way to overcome the "Vocabulary Problem" ... showing different users use different terms to describe the same things. (37)

However, as we pointed out in part I, the socially related advantages of tags only apply to social settings in which multiple tags are shared. Such advantages are nullified if users exploit tags for their own personal information management rather than for social information behaviors (Pak, Pautz, and Iden 2007).

Tags in Current PIM Systems

In recent years, tags have diffused from content-sharing systems to PIM systems and are currently integrated into personal systems for managing web favorites, emails, and files.

Web Favorites

Delicious (mentioned in chapter 3) is web-based bookmarking software that uses tags instead of folders. It is both a PIM tool, because users can bookmark web pages for their own personal use, and a Web 2.0 tool, because it allows users to share their web favorites with other users across the Internet.

Emails

Google's Gmail, first introduced in 2004, supplied users with what were termed *labels*. At first, Gmail allowed users to use labels only as tags (hereafter *tag-labels*); users could (and still can) add as many tag-labels as they wanted to an email, thus allowing multiple classification. This tag-label method did not move emails from the single repository where they were contained—that is, the inbox (see figure 6.1). Beginning in 2009, Gmail also allowed users to use labels as folders (hereafter *folder-labels*). With folder-labels, participants can drag emails from the inbox "into" a label (see figure 6.2). Folder-labels are single classification, because an email receives only one tag. After being dragged to a label, the email disappears from the inbox and loses its "Inbox" tag; moreover, if dragged into a second label, it loses the previous one. As with folders, the user needs to "open" the

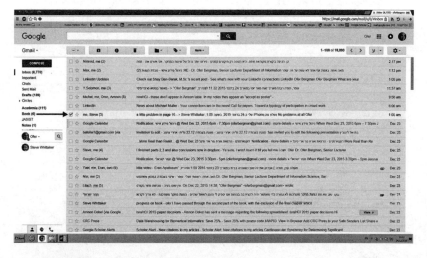

Figure 6.1
Tag-labeling in Gmail.

Figure 6.2
Folder-labeling in Gmail.

label and go through the messages it "contains" in order to
retrieve the information needed. Therefore, Gmail users currently have two ways of using labels: tag-labeling, in which
labels are dragged to an email, and folder-labeling, in which
emails are dragged into labels. Regardless of the way that they
are categorized, there are two ways of retrieving email: by using
a location (i.e., opening a label in a folder-navigation-like way)
or by using non-location-based search (via either tags or other
search words).

Files

Microsoft introduced tags into its operating system in Windows
Vista along with the traditional file folders hierarchy, and tags
were retained in Windows 7, 8, and 10. Files can be stored either
in a single repository (e.g., My Documents) or in designated

subfolders with as many tags as users choose to assign to the file. Users have three different options for using tags for retrieval: by using search (with one or more tags as keywords), in combination with folder navigation (sorting the folder by tags), and via the "arrange by" option (arranging the files in a collection by tags instead of by folders).

Users' Attitudes toward Tagging

In a study comparing tags with folders (Bergman et al. 2013b), we first tested users' attitudes toward tagging. One hundred and sixty-eight participants answered our questionnaire. Participants tended to express positive attitudes toward tagging: 77 percent of our participants thought that "giving several classifications to personal information" was a good idea, 72 percent agreed that "in 20 years children born today will use mostly tags," and 61 percent agreed with the claim that "most people use folders only due to habits." Our results indicate that when asked hypothetically about their attitudes, computer users tend to agree with those PIM researchers who support the tag everything approach— but what is their actual behavior? Do users prefer tags to folders when *actually* managing their personal information? Before reporting how we tested this, we will review previous literature that compares folder usage with tag usage.

Comparison between Folder and Tag Usage

Several laboratory studies have compared folder and tag usage in PIM. Five studies compared folder use to their own tagging prototypes, testing for storage time, retrieval time, retrieval errors, and number of mouse clicks: Quan et al. (2003); Ma and

Wiedenbeck (2009); Voit, Andrews, and Slany (2012); Hsieh et al. (2008); and Sajedi, Afzali, and Zabardast (2012). In addition to efficiency and success, three other studies also tested cognitive load and degree of frustration (Civan et al. 2008; Gao 2001; Pak, Pautz, and Iden 2007). A summary of the results of these eight articles is presented in table 6.1.

Table 6.1 shows mixed results regarding almost all comparisons between folders and tags, giving no clear indication that tag usage is superior to folder usage. All eight studies used controlled tasks in which users carried out experimenter-generated filing and retrieval tasks. As we have noted previously, although this methodology has important advantages (including control over materials), it does not use participants' own personal information, which is a critical aspect of PIM. Moreover, none of these studies allowed participants to *choose* whether to exploit folders or tags so as to express their preferences via real choice behavior. Instead, preferences were inferred from user ratings. Finally, none of these studies examined participants' choices related to single or multiple classification.

Prior to our own research (Bergman et al. 2013a), we were aware of just one study that assessed users' choices for tags versus folders in a natural setting. However, this study still did not evaluate users' behavior regarding multiple versus single classification. The study was performed by two members of the Google research team that introduced folder-like Gmail labels (Rodden and Leggett 2010). The change was introduced because "while the flexibility and power of labels was appreciated by the users who discovered them, labels were often not discoverable or understandable for another set of users, who would have been happy with the simpler solution of folders" (4588). The Google team introduced folder labels to millions of users, and unlike

Table 6.1

Summary of papers testing folders vs. tags for efficiency, cognitive load, and frustration level (exp means experiment)

	Folders are better	No substantial/ significant difference	Tags are better
Storage			
Time	Voit, Andrews, and Slany 2012; Pak, Pautz, and Iden 2007 (exp2);	Sajedi, Afzali, and Zabardast 2012; Ma and Wiedenbeck 2009	Quan et al. 2003; Pak, Pautz, and Iden 2007 (exp1)
Mouse clicks/ physical difficulty	Civan et al. 2008	Pak, Pautz, and Iden 2007 (exp2)	
Cognitive load	Gao 2011	Pak, Pautz, and Iden 2007 (exp1, 2)	Civan et al. 2008
Frustration	Pak, Pautz, and Iden 2007 (exp1); Gao 2011		
Retrieval			
Time		Voit, Andrews, and Slany 2012; Ma and Wiedenbeck 2009; Civan et al. 2008; Gao 2011	Hsieh et al. 2008; Sajedi, Afzali, and Zabardast 2012; Quan et al. 2003
Errors	Gao 2011		Sajedi, Afzali, and Zabardast 2012;
Mouse clicks	Hsieh et al. 2008	Gao 2011	Voit, Andrews, and Slany, 2012; Ma and Wiedenbeck 2009; Pak, Pautz, and Iden 2007 (exp2)
Cognitive load	Gao 2011 (secondary task)	Gao 2011 (subjective evaluation)	

most studies that have relatively small samples of participants, the Google results were derived from a vast population that used Gmail for everyday work. Results showed that when given the new possibility of folder-labeling, users' chances of creating labels doubled, and the percentage of folder-label storage exceeded that of tag-label storage. The researchers therefore concluded that "with this design, the team expects that users will be able to discover and use the more advanced aspects of labeling (such as multiple inclusion) at the point where they identify a need, but it will be important to verify that" (4595). Our research tests exactly that conjecture; however, unlike Rodden and Leggett (2010), we made sure that our participants were aware of both tag-label and folder-label options so that our results could not be explained by users' ignorance.

Evaluating the Tag Everything Approach

The main purpose of our study (Bergman et al. 2013a) was to test users' preferences for folders versus tags in PIM environments (Gmail and Windows 7) that support both folders and tags. This testing was performed in several ways: (a) directly, by observing actual folder- and tag-related behaviors; (b) by testing single versus multiple classification behaviors; and (c) by studying hierarchical versus nonhierarchical behavior. In addition, we tested the retrieval efficiency of the two methods.

We used a multimethod research design: we ran two studies in two different environments to increase the generalizability of our results. Furthermore, to increase the convergent validity of our findings, we collected different types of data (quantitative and qualitative) using surveys, experimental manipulation, and natural observations. We conducted two studies: the Gmail study, to test email management preferences; and the Windows 7 study, to test preferences regarding file management. In both studies, we exposed our participants to folders and tags, putting a special emphasis on explaining multiple classification.

In the Gmail study, we examined the mailboxes of our twenty-three participants for folder and tag-labeling behavior after a month during which they could use whichever method they chose. Participants also answered a questionnaire regarding their retrieval habits.

In the Windows 7 study, we asked our twenty-three participants to use tags instead of folders for two weeks (*forced tagging activity*), conducted a controlled retrieval task, and then returned five weeks later to test users' folder or tag preferences after a period during which they managed their folders as they chose (*free choice activity*). In this study, we also used specially developed classification recording software that allowed us to scan the participants' file systems and that recorded the storage location and number of tags attached to each file. We used this software three times: (1) before the forced tagging activity; (2) after the forced tagging activity, as a manipulation check; and (3) after the free choice activity. The manipulation check indicated that participants had complied with our instructions (on average, they tagged 71 percent of the files accessed and used multiple classification in 55 percent of their tagged files). In addition, we used a retrieval questionnaire and interviewed participants, asking them to explain their behaviors. Unlike the majority of the previous literature testing for folder or tag preference, both studies were conducted in naturalistic settings; that is, participants managed their own information items on their own computers as part of their daily routine. This factor argues for the greater ecological validity of our results.

Overall, our study results show a strong preference for folders over tags, for single over multiple classification, for hierarchical over flat storage, and for location-based over non-location-based retrieval, as detailed in the following sections.

Folders vs. Tags
Results showed a strong preference for folder over tag usage in PIM for both storage and retrieval. Regarding storage, 67 percent of all labeled messages in the Gmail study were folder-labeled, compared to 33 percent tagged-labeled (confirming Rodden and Leggett [2010]). Moreover, the main reported reason for tagging behavior was a wish to keep emails visible in the inbox rather than a need for multiple classifications. We elaborated in chapter 3 on how users tend to keep their actionable messages in the inbox in order to see and be reminded of them. In the Windows 7 study, 96 percent of files were stored in specific folders (rather than default ones), and only six participants (16 percent) tagged any of their files during the test phase (two of the participants tagged only a single file each). Retrieval results are even more striking: In the Gmail study, an average of 16 percent of retrievals was estimated to be conducted by opening a folder-label, compared to only 3 percent using tag search. In the Windows 7 study, participants estimated that they used navigation for 61 percent of their retrievals, compared to just 5 percent for tag retrieval. Thus, our findings are unequivocal, in contrast to previous studies (see table 6.1) that presented ambiguous results regarding the superiority of one approach or the other (for storage as well as retrieval). Based on users' behaviors, we found that most prefer folders for storage and for retrieval. Similar strong preferences for folders compared with tags for email retrieval were shown for logfile data in Whittaker et al. (2011), in which

folders were used for 12 percent of retrievals and tags for just 1 percent.

Although these results are striking, we should reiterate that they don't apply to tagging of web resources, for which users may benefit from social tagging (as noted in chapter 3). In addition, user behavior is often determined by long-term experience and habit, which might have affected participants' choices when one system or the other dominated their past experience. We aimed to overcome this possible habit effect in the Windows 7 study by successfully forcing our participants to tag for two weeks prior to the experimental task. Nevertheless, we are aware that in spite of our efforts, long-term habits may still affect behavior, and participants' choices still may be at least partly affected by past experience. As tags increasingly are deployed and users without previous experience are exposed to both systems, future studies may be less influenced by this possible habit effect.

Single vs. Multiple Classification

Many PIM researchers have criticized the hierarchical approach for limiting users to a single classification (Dourish et al. 2000; Lansdale 1988; Hsieh et al. 2008; Bloehdorn and Völkel 2006; Marsden and Cairns 2003; Quan et al. 2003; Heckner, Heilemann, and Wolff 2009; Rodden and Leggett 2010). However, our results indicate that when given the choice, users clearly prefer single classification and rarely use multiple classification. We explored these questions for both storage and retrieval. For storage, in the Gmail study, 92 percent of the labeled emails on average had a single label, compared to only 8 percent with multiple labels for tag-labeling participants. In the Windows 7 study, only six participants used tags, so no conclusions regarding multiple classification could be drawn (but perhaps if participants were more enthusiastic regarding multiple classification, then more of them would have used tags). Results regarding retrieval were more clear-cut: In the Gmail study, participants estimated that only one message out of a thousand was retrieved by using multiple labels, and in the Windows 7 study, participants (including the six who used tags for storage) stated that they *never* used multiple classification for retrieval.

There are several possible explanations for a single classification preference:

Multiple classification may be difficult and time consuming. This idea was suggested by our results; almost half of the participants in the Windows 7 study indicated that tagging was either difficult or time consuming. If standard classification into single folders is cognitively challenging (Lansdale 1988; Malone 1983; Dumais and Landauer 1983), then (contrary to prior theorists' views) multiple classification may *increase* this difficulty. In situations in which several possible classifications immediately come to the user's mind, multiple classification may indeed eliminate the cognitive cost of selection, but in other situations thinking of a single category may be simpler than attempting to think of all possible ones. In addition, Pak, Pautz, and Iden (2007) suggest that classification by tags is cognitively more demanding because tags tend to be item-specific, whereas folder classification tends to be more generic. Moreover, the flexibility of tagging usage may turn out to be a disadvantage; the fact that ordinary end users are untrained in indexing, the lack of vocabulary control, and the ambiguous nature of language can lead to inconsistency in tagging, and this in turn may affect the efficiency of later information retrieval (Gao 2011).

Single classification is sufficient. Some of our participants as well as those reported in previous studies (Civan et al. 2008; Quan et al. 2003; Wash and Radar 2007) felt that multiple tags may be redundant and that one category was sufficient for use in retrieving information items. This is also consistent with our other work examining retrieval using traditional single-classification folders. In Bergman et al.'s 2008 study, participants estimated that they remember the exact location of 74 percent to 90 percent of their files on average (depending on the study). In Bergman et al.'s 2010 study, participants were able to retrieve 94 percent of their files using navigation, and only 6 percent of files were not found at all. Therefore, although navigation may not be perfect, it may be sufficient for the majority of users.

Multiple categorization makes exhaustive retrieval inefficient. This view was advanced by one of the participants in the study by Civan et al. (2008): "You can exhaustively search a set of folders, you can search one folder and if it's not there, you search the next folder and so on. But you can't do the same thing with labels because they overlap so much and you don't want to look at the same things over and over again. That makes search inefficient and redundant" (10).

In summary, we suggest that single classification is preferred because it is simpler than multiple classification. It is reasonable to assume that a one-to-one relationship (information item *a* is in folder *x*) is easier to remember than a one-to-many relationship (information item *a* can be retrieved by using tags *x*, *y*, or *z*). This view was expressed by one of the participants in the Windows 7 study: "Multiple tags are somewhat cumbersome. One short name for a tag is something that can be remembered and eases retrieval" (Bergman et al. 2013a). Future cognitive research should test this hypothesis in a controlled laboratory environment.

Hierarchical vs. Flat Storage

Both of our studies indicated a preference for the hierarchical method over flat storage and non-location-based retrieval. Regarding storage, in the Gmail study, 79 percent of participants indicated that they would prefer a hierarchical labeling system over the current flat one. In the Windows 7 study, participants stored 86 percent of their files in a nonflat, hierarchical location. Indeed, in April 2010, as part of Google Labs (a presentation of experimental features), Gmail introduced nested labels—the ability to create a hierarchical label structure. The Gmail blog noted that "a highly requested feature for labels, though, comes from the world of folders: the ability to organize labels hierarchically."[1] Following users' feedback, nested labels became a standard feature in the new Gmail interface released in June 2011.

Location-Based vs. Non-Location-Based Retrieval

On average, participants estimated that they used navigation for 69 percent of their retrievals in the Gmail study and 61 percent in the Windows 7 study and used non-location-based retrieval for the remainder (31 percent and 39 percent, respectively), indicating that introducing users to tags did not induce non-location-based retrieval. These results are in line with previous research. In Jones, Phuwanartnurak, et al. (2005), participants refused to relinquish their folders, even hypothetically. Gao (2011) stated that "the hierarchical structure of categorization may encourage or force users to form a clear mental structure of the information" (826). The large-scale study (Bergman et al. 2010) described in chapter 4 also found that participants retrieved their files from hierarchical folders with very little use of default storage locations such as My Documents, and as we indicated in chapter 5, participants estimated that they navigated to their files in the majority of their retrievals regardless of the search engine they had available. Finally, Teevan et al. (2004) found a strong preference for retrieval in steps, from the general to the specific (i.e., *orienteering*). This approach is well-supported by folder navigation, but not by tag retrieval (Gao 2011).

Retrieval Efficiency

Our controlled retrieval task results also did not find tag retrieval to be more efficient than other forms of retrieval. On the contrary, it resulted in more retrieval failures and significantly slower retrievals. These results do not conform with those of Hsieh et al. (2008) and Quan et al. (2003), but they are in line with our own findings (Bergman et al. 2010), mentioned earlier. One possible reason for the discrepancy between results may be that our work explored naturalistic tasks in which participants retrieved files from their own file systems, whereas other studies used artificial materials.

Tags as Cognitive Nodes in a Concept Network

The results of our study indicate that with regard to PIM, participants prefer folders over tags and single over multiple classification, both for storage and retrieval. Participants also prefer location-based over non-location-based retrieval. Perceived simplicity might explain these preferences. However, according to Hsieh et al. (2008), simplicity should cause the opposite result. Recall that Hsieh et al. argue that tags are more compatible with human cognition, in which semantic processing is based on a flat-structure tag network (Collins and Loftus 1975). However, just because the tag-like model is similar to our *internal* cognitive representations, it does not logically follow that tags are the best model for *externally* storing our personal information. This may reflect a conceptual confusion regarding the objectives of organizing information. The main aim of information item classification in PIM is not to externalize our internal representation of these items (Hsieh et al. 2008) or to fully describe them, as implied by Civan et al. (2008), but to support easy, fast, and efficient retrieval. Therefore, the comparison between organizational methods should not focus on theoretical discussions about which organization more closely mimics our cognitive system or which gives a more exhaustive description of a relevant information item. Instead, evaluations should focus on critical retrieval and storage parameters, such as users' preferences, retrieval speed, and accuracy.

Summary

Tags are popular for Web 2.0 content sharing. However, our study showed that when it comes to managing and retrieving their own personal information, users prefer folders over tags and make little use of multiple classification. Tags have been shown to be helpful in content-sharing Web 2.0 contexts, but in such settings there are huge numbers of information items and users cannot possibly know where every item is located. In PIM, on the other hand, users are very familiar with their own information organization; after all, they stored items in their system according to their own subjective needs (Bergman, Beyth-Marom, and Nachmias 2003, 2008). Therefore, in the great majority of PIM cases, users can retrieve their own personal information quickly and efficiently without the need to generate multiple retrieval labels (Bergman et al. 2010).

7 The Group Management Alternative

In the previous chapter, we discussed the success of tags as a way to organize shared information on the web. Applications like Delicious allow individual users to tag web resources, applying labels that can be shared. Those shared tags may then help others to find relevant web resources (Millen, Feinberg, and Kerr 2006). In part I of the book, we introduced a new approach to PIM known as group information management (GIM), which also allows information sharing. In GIM (Erickson 2006), personal information organization and retrieval strategies are partially delegated to others—exploiting others' organization to assist with PIM goals. This method is now becoming more important with the increased use of collaborative repositories such as Dropbox, Google Drive, and OneDrive, which now have millions of users (Massey, Lennig, and Whittaker 2014). Modern work is inherently collaborative (Bellotti et al. 2005; Whittaker 2005; Hinds 2002), with the consequence that users are often required to share online resources. This chapter explores whether using others' organization via GIM might address PIM problems by allowing users to find shared resources that have been structured by others without those users having to organize resources personally.

When a group of two or more people start collaborating, they typically face the dilemma of how to share the files they create together. Groups need to choose between distributing files as email attachments and then storing them in *personal repositories* or storing shared files in a *common repository* (e.g., using cloud-based services such as Google Drive or Dropbox). If they choose email distribution and personal repositories, each person in the group can organize the files in their own way. We therefore refer to such a system as PIM. If they choose a common repository, the group first needs to agree on the files' organization; this then is GIM.

There are excellent theoretical arguments for using GIM as an alternative to PIM for group-related files. PIM requires additional work; each collaborator has to independently manage his or her own personal collection of shared files, thus duplicating files, time, and cognitive effort. Furthermore, there may be significant problems involved in retrieving, managing, and reconciling different versions of a document when multiple versions are distributed through email to multiple participants (Ducheneaut and Bellotti 2001; Whittaker, Bellotti, and Gwizdka 2007). Many organizations therefore have a policy of encouraging their teams to use a common repository when sharing files (Matthews et al. 2013).

This chapter reports on the first study that directly compares retrieval using GIM and PIM for file sharing in a naturalistic setting (Bergman, Whittaker, and Falk 2014): We asked 275 users to retrieve 860 of their shared files and tested the effect of sharing method (PIM vs. GIM) on different retrieval measures (success and efficiency). We also tested the effect on retrieval success and efficiency of different storage options (storing files in default folders vs. storing them in specific user-created ones), as well as folder depth and other independent variables.

Group Information Management

In GIM, two or more collaborators share files using a common repository. Typically, collaborators develop these files together. The common repository can be located on an intranet server (if all members of the group belong to the same organization) or in the cloud, giving collaborators ubiquitous access to shared files by using any device with Internet access.

In one of the first papers exploring GIM, Berlin et al. (1993) report their personal experiences in developing a collaborative repository for long-term files they commonly used, including meeting notes, design documents, and bug work-arounds. They began optimistically: "We expected to sit down, agree on a single, simple classification, and be done. Given our similar project goals, computing environment, and research interests, our only concern was that we were too homogeneous to have interesting differences in personal styles. We were wrong. Very wrong" (25). The authors experienced many problems in structuring their collaborative document space resulting from multifaceted individual differences in organizational style. Among the individual differences they found were those between (a) *purists* who preferred to store each file in a single location versus *proliferators* who preferred to store files in all possible locations; (b) *syntactists* who based their structure on episodic cues and the context in which the information was used versus *semanticists* who based their organization on document meaning; (c) *scruffies* who wanted "only five" top-level categories versus *neatniks* who wanted "three hundred fine-grained" folders; and (d) *savers* who wanted to keep all possibly relevant documents versus *deleters* who thought that doing so would create clutter and thus wanted to keep a minimal set of documents.

Possibly as a result of these differences in organizational style, Berlin et al. report that when attempting to retrieve a document, members of the group experienced major problems. They tried to guess other members' idiosyncratic organizational style but often failed to do so correctly. This problem was also described by Lutters, Ackerman, and Zhou (2007) as follows: "People adding and retrieving information in group information systems must mash their often idiosyncratic categories, indices, schema and information routines" (243). A possible reason for this mismatch is that people are experienced at naming folders for their own use but not at doing so when they are collaborating with others.

Another early study by Whittaker (1996) identified different types of problems with collaborative repositories. He conducted interviews and analyzed logfile data for long-term users of Lotus Notes, a work-based collaborative repository that allowed participants to share files, post comments, and engage in structured online conversations. Participants in that study were reluctant to adopt Lotus Notes, observing that their collaborators were often unaware of when new materials had been added to the common repository. To alert others about new content, participants sent emails notifying others about repository changes, sometimes including the new documents as attachments in those emails. This undermined the common repository, leading some group members to abandon it and rely solely on email for sharing documents. More recent work on enterprise sharing tools reveals similar alerting issues (Mahmud et al. 2011; Voida et al. 2006). Two systems—TeleNotes (Whittaker et al. 1997) and Topika (Mahmud et al. 2011)—attempt to remedy this problem by incorporating user-configurable email alerting as the repository is updated. Another prototype that addresses the problem of alerting is Sharing Palette (Voida et al. 2006). However, none of these systems has been widely adopted, and effective alerting remains a difficult problem. On the one hand, collaborators need systematic alerting to avoid overlooking relevant updates to the repository. On the other, sending too many alerts leads to information overload, making it difficult to determine which alerts are important.

In a qualitative study, Rader (2009) found that there is little feeling of common ownership in shared repositories. In a paper titled "Yours, Mine and (Not) Ours," she described how her participants restricted activities to *their own* files in a common repository and were careful not to delete files that possibly might be useful to others. As a result, the repository became cluttered and poorly organized, and participants wasted time and effort when attempting to find information, especially information created by others. One of her participants said: "Probably the biggest problem we have with CTools is that people tend to organize information [in] different ways" (2096). Similar failures to agree on a common organizational structure are reported in recent enterprise sharing tools (Muller, Millen, and Feinberg 2010; Shami, Muller, and Millen 2011).

In another qualitative study, Voida, Olson, and Olson (2013) report their participants' misconceptions about three elements of common repositories: (a) different cloud-based services with different affordances; (b) different digital identifiers that reflect different facets of individual identity; and (c) different collaborators with different work practices. These differences and the interactions between them made cloud-based management so complex that one participant commented: "When I try to wrap my head around all my different documents ... It kind of makes my head hurt to think about it" (1).

One exception to these observations of failed collaborative tools is a recent qualitative study by Massey et al. (2014), which is unusual in that it examines collaborative tools used by participants outside academia (twenty-seven high-tech workers). The authors identified a set of successful strategies used with collaborative tools, including creating explicit metadata descriptions with links to shared resources, as well as implicit strategies that rely on knowledge of other team members' expertise, task workflows, and tool affordances. However, these strategies were found in small teams and may not scale well to larger team collaborations.

A final problem with collaborative file sharing relates to version control: If two (or more) collaborators make synchronous changes to different versions of a file, then the two (or more) versions need to be merged into a third version. To avoid this complication, it is important that each collaborator works on the latest version of the file. Therefore, collaborators need to agree on a common versioning method, but often fail to do so because each collaborator has his or her own versioning scheme; for example, one collaborator may use numbers, whereas another may use dates (Karlson, Smith, and Lee 2011). This issue seems to be more problematic with common repositories than email, as articulated by one study participant: "The idea of having two [versions of] organizing schemes being applied to the same folder at the same time is disturbing to me. So I wouldn't do it. I'd email it to him and say: put it where you want it to be" (2674). On the other hand, current cloud-based sharing applications such as Google Drive may eliminate the need to create different versions of files (and the need to coordinate edits) by allowing multiple collaborators to coedit a file simultaneously. Our study did not address the file-sharing versioning problem, but we will return to this issue when we discuss future GIM research at the end of this chapter.

Regardless of these problems, cloud-based storage and sharing applications such as Google Drive, Dropbox, Amazon Cloud Drive, Apple's iCloud, and Microsoft's OneDrive are showing rapid adoption (Massey et al. 2014). Cloud-based computing is projected to overtake local storage by 2020 (Anderson and Rainie 2012), with pervasive network access and support for concurrent editing being positive reasons for adoption (Park and Ryoo 2012). The main aim of our study (Bergman, Whittaker, and Falk 2014) was to systematically compare the effectiveness of common versus personal repositories for supporting retrieval.

Retrieval Is More Effective for Personally Organized Files

We examined retrieval using the elicited personal information retrieval (EPIR) method, which was explained in chapter 4 (Bergman, Tene-Rubinstein, and Shalom 2013; Bergman et al. 2010; Bergman et al. 2013a). Participants retrieved files that other users had shared during naturally occurring collaborations. Thus, participants were free to choose their sharing, storage, and retrieval methods when retrieving files from their own computers. As noted before, this naturalistic approach increased the ecological validity of the research compared with more lab-based techniques (Civan et al. 2008; Fitchett, Cockburn, and Gutwin 2013; Gao 2011; Pak, Pautz, and Iden 2007). Although we gathered data from each participant individually, it was important for us to gather it from a large number of participants ($N = 275$) to increase external validity.

Our procedure involved identifying a list of files that other collaborators had shared with each participant. The testers therefore used a participant's computer desktop search engine to search each participant's computer for files for which the file author's name was different that the participant's user name. Because many cloud storage services keep a local copy of the shared folder on the computer of each person who shares that folder (e.g., Dropbox does so by default and Google Drive upon request), the desktop search engine captured (and our lists included) both GIM files and PIM files. During testing, the tester looked at the location of each candidate file and excluded it from the retrieval list if it was in the same folder as previously searched-for files. Such files were excluded because pilot results showed that folder duplication primed retrievals, which could bias our results.

When using this method, we looked for document files (rather than music or picture files), because people typically collaborate using documents. In each retrieval task, the tester asked the participant to retrieve a single shared file by specifying its name. Participants were instructed to retrieve the target file and click on it once but not open it (to retain the participant's privacy). Each retrieval attempt continued until the file was successfully found or the participant said he or she could not find it. Retrieval was screenrecorded via software residing on a USB memory stick that did not require installation. Participants were not confined to a specific retrieval method; they could choose how to retrieve the file (e.g., they might choose to either navigate or search). However, participants were not allowed to directly copy the file name into their desktop search boxes, because this would not have been a realistic simulation of retrieval; real-life search processes are clearly cognitive in nature, requiring participants to actively generate search terms (Ingw-ersen 1996). After the retrieval task, we administered a survey that addressed participants' sharing preferences.

Sharing Methods: Reasons PIM Is Preferred and More Efficient

Our study found a strong preference to share files via email (thus performing PIM) rather than via a cloud-based or organizational shared repository (GIM). Participants estimated that on average they use email to share 86 percent of their files with others and to receive 65 percent of files created by other users. Preference for email attachments over using a shared repository was also reported previously (Rader 2007; Whittaker 1996; Voida et al. 2006). However, our study also explored reasons for this preference. Our novel findings indicate that from a retrieval perspective, users' preference for email sharing and PIM over cloud-based sharing and GIM seems rational. When using GIM, users' chance of failing to find a file (22 percent) was significantly higher than when using PIM (13 percent). Using PIM instead of GIM makes sense; although with PIM each person in the collaboration needs to classify and manage a shared file individually, this additional effort substantially increases the chances of finding that shared file.

When we explored this finding more deeply, we identified a possible explanation for these GIM failures. We compared retrieval success and efficiency of cloud-based shared files stored in folders created by the participants themselves with those created by others. We found that the failure rate from shared folders created by others (28 percent) is more than five times higher than that of retrievals from shared folders created by participants themselves (5 percent). Furthermore, the retrieval time from such other-created shared folders is also significantly higher. It therefore seems that the root of the problem is not cloud storage and GIM itself but the fact that other people created the folder. Moreover, the failure rate for shared folders created by others is also significantly higher than retrievals from default folders, such as My Documents and Dropbox root directories (17 percent), indicating that using other people's organization leads to worse results than using no organization at all.

Why do people remember the location of their files better using PIM than using GIM? We suggest four possible reasons:

The subjectivity of classification: The category that an information item is allocated to (i.e., the folder where it is placed) is not directly derivable from the information item itself (Kwasnik 1991; Bergman, Beyth-Marom, and Nachmias 2003). Our data indicates that there is a substantial amount of subjectivity (user dependence) in categorization; users were substantially less successful in finding files that other people had categorized. In the words of participant 212: "I can't follow the associative thinking of other people"(1956) Similar results were obtained by Berlin et al. (1993); Lutters, Ackerman, and Zhou (2007); Rader (2009); and Voida, Olson, and Olson (2013). The subjectivity of classification is explored in detail in part III of the book.

Constructivism: Constructivism is a well-established theory in the field of education. It argues against older accounts of learning as passive absorption of information. Instead, it suggests that learners actively reconstruct information using their own mental structures and prior knowledge. It also claims that active learning is more effective (Twomey and Maarten 1996). The benefits of active information processing to facilitate later memory is also shown in educational settings. When students actively summarize educational videos (Bergman et al. 2000) or lectures

(Kalnikaité and Whittaker 2007), their memories improve and the retrieval of information is more efficient. As noted in chapter 3, active classification has also repeatedly been shown to promote recall in many memory studies (Craik and Lockhart 1972; Schacter 2008). In the PIM context, we observed that the act of creating folders and actively organizing information items into them engages thinking about these information items, and this in turn aids retrieval (Bergman, Beyth-Marom, and Nachmias 2003; Jones, Phuwanartnurak, et al. 2005). In GIM, on the other hand, most of the "pain" of categorization is omitted because categorization is performed by other collaborators. The consequence in common repositories is that participants lose the "gain" of familiarity with information and its organization. As a result, retrieval is more error-prone and less efficient in GIM settings.

Episodic memory: Cognitive psychology distinguishes two types of explicit memories: *Semantic memory* is our long-term knowledge of the world and is independent of the way that knowledge was acquired (e.g., I know that Paris is the capital of France even if I don't remember where I learned this information), and *episodic memory* is memory of our own experiences (e.g., I was in Paris last spring). Episodic cues have been shown to benefit retrieval (Linton 1982; Wagenaar 1994). When retrieving PIM information, people can rely not only on semantic memory but also on episodic memory (i.e., specific memories of the occasion and context in which the document was stored, such as remembering working on a document over the holidays). Moreover, in PIM, even if the purpose of a folder has changed and users can no longer rely on semantic clues, they still may remember storing an information item in that folder and may use this episodic memory for the item's retrieval. In GIM, how-ever, information in many cases is not stored by a user but by his or her collaborators, and thus users do not have access to such experiential cues about the context of storage. If others store information for us, then potentially important episodic cues are lost. In part III, we will discuss designs for novel PIM technologies that explicitly attempt to capture this episodic context.

Locus of control: In PIM, people control the way in which they organize their information. However, in GIM this control is necessarily limited, because organization is generated in part by others. In GIM, people also need to consider other peoples' requirements and group decisions, even when organizing files themselves. It is well-known in experimental psychology that reduced control over a situation decreases both motivation and task performance (Ajzen 2002).

Note that the latter three arguments may also be relevant for automatic classification. In *automatic classification*, an applica-tion attempts to learn a user's subjective classification so as to classify information for that user (Agrawal, Bayardo, and Srikant 2000; Maes 1994). However, even if such automatic classifica-tion is completely accurate, retrieval may be problematic because (a) users are not active in the classification process, and this pas-sivity may compromise later memory; (b) as with GIM, users have no episodic memory of the classification; and (c) users may feel that they are not in control of their own personal informa-tion organization—which may result in negative feelings regard-less of retrieval success. We discuss automatic classification in chapter 13.

Storage Methods: Personal Storage Effort Pays Off

The notion of "no pain, no gain" is also strongly supported by our findings regarding storage methods. If a person does not actively categorize information themselves, then the chances of finding that information reduce significantly. Retrievals from user-created folders were significantly better than retrievals from general default folders as measured by failure percent, percent of missteps, and retrieval time. To successfully and efficiently find files, it is not enough to share those files via email. Instead, one must make the additional effort of categorizing information. Malone's (1983) research on physical offices found qualitative evidence that filers were more efficient at retrieving their documents than pilers. In contrast, as we saw in chapter 4, Whittaker et al. (2011) did not find that emails in folders were retrieved more efficiently or successfully than emails stored in their general default location, which is the inbox. Our findings concur with Malone, rather than Whittaker et al. However, the reduced success of active email filing may result from the fact that alternative retrieval methods such as search and sorting are more straightforward in email, because messages contain more salient metadata (sender, reply to, etc.) than is available for personal files.

In our GIM study, the mean hierarchical depth of shared files stored in specific user-created folders (2.2 folders deep) was similar to that found by Bergman et al. (2010) for personal files. Also consistent with Bergman et al. (2010), we also found a positive correlation between a file's depth and retrieval time. This correlation makes sense, as each step down the hierarchy tree takes time. However, in our current study we found that GIM files were stored deeper in the folder hierarchy than PIM files stored on the local drive. Why should people store GIM files deeper in their hierarchies? One possible reason is that when creating GIM structures, people are more elaborate (e.g., dividing a folder into subfolders to create a clearer organization), because they are worried that others may not be able to find information. Another possible reason is that unlike PIM, GIM hierarchies such as those in Dropbox and Google Drive do not provide users with desktop storage, which is commonly exploited by PIM users. One consequence of this greater depth is increased GIM retrieval time (Bergman et al. 2010). Future research might explore these different explanations for the greater depth of GIM files.

A Full Comparison between PIM and GIM

Cloud storage is rapidly being adopted for group collaboration, because it allows for ubiquitous retrieval and device-independent backup. However, the fact that cloud-based file sharing is more modern and trendy than using email attachments does not necessarily mean that it is *better* in terms of retrieval. Our results justify users' preference for PIM-based methods of sharing files via email attachments over GIM cloud-based file sharing. A PIM strategy significantly increases users' chances of finding their files, in particular if each user stores a file in his or her own user-created folder. Thus, from the retrieval perspective, the redundancy of each person performing his or her own PIM for different versions of the same shared files is not a waste of time and energy.

There are other advantages of PIM over GIM for group collaboration:

Agreement on a collaborative tool: Our qualitative data indicates other possible advantages of email sharing over cloud-based sharing. Email is a reliable lowest common denominator system; sharing via email does not require all collaborators to use the same email application, so a Microsoft Outlook user has no problems sharing file attachments with a Gmail user, for example. In contrast, sharing files in the cloud requires agreement to use a shared system; Dropbox users cannot share files with Google Drive users.

Agreement on organization scheme: Cloud-based sharing also requires agreement and coordination regarding the way the files are organized (Berlin et al. 1993; Rader 2009; Lutters, Ackerman, and Zhou 2007), whereas email file sharing does not.

Control: PIM participants felt more in control of their files. This makes sense; in a shared repository, other participants can make unwanted changes to a file or even accidentally delete it (Rader 2009). In contrast, the sender always has the original version of the file when using email.

Alerting: Rader's (2009) participants stressed the need to be informed of updates in the shared repository. Some of our participants preferred email sharing because alerting was more reliable; they knew that their recipients would be checking their email regularly, which was not always true of collaborative repositories. Others also liked the fact that email alerting allowed them to add contextual information to the file in the message, such as motivations for file changes or outstanding tasks. However, Voida, Olsen, and Olsen (2013), consistent with prior work (e.g., Gutwin, Roseman, and Greenberg 1996), note that alerting is a complex design issue. Some cloud designs provide insufficient alerting information, whereas others provide too much. Solving the alerting problem automatically is extremely hard. How can an application determine whether an update is meaningful or important to a specific person? In email, there is no such problem; users send their collaborators a version when they feel that it is significantly better than the previous one.

However, GIM also has some advantages over PIM:

Simultaneous work: To avoid complex versioning problems, collaborators using email need to take turns when working on a file. In contrast, some cloud-based facilities such as Google Drive and SharePoint allow several collaborators to simultaneously work on the same file.

Email overload: Computer users repeatedly complain about email overload (Dabbish et al. 2005; Whittaker 2011; Whittaker and Sidner 1996), and PIM sharing clearly contributes to this by increasing the number of messages sent and received.

Table 7.1 summarizes comparisons between PIM (email-based file sharing) and GIM (cloud-based file sharing).

From an organizational point of view, one behavioral implication of our findings might be to discourage groups of workers from sharing files in the cloud or to limit cloud sharing to a few files that are constantly updated in parallel by a group of workers (e.g., a bug list).

Implications for Design

One significant design implication for GIM might be to allow simultaneous editing but preserve personal organization. A shared file could be stored in the cloud, allowing simultaneous work, but each participant could organize it in his or her own folder according to individual categorization schemes.

Table 7.1

Comparison between PIM and GIM file sharing, showing advantages of PIM for almost all dimensions ($a > b$ means *a is better than b*)

	PIM/email	Advantage	GIM/cloud
Failed retrievals rate	13%	>	22%
Agreement on collaborative tool	No need	>	Necessary
Agreement on organization scheme	No need	>	Needed for retrieval
Control	Sender has original and can accept/reject changes	>	Typically, user has no control over changes and deletions others make
Alerting	User-controlled; noticeable notification because users check their email constantly; perceived as more reliable, simple, and contextualized	>	Too often, too weak, too technical; perceived as less reliable and more complicated
Simultaneous work	Not possible	<	Allows simultaneous work (in Google Drive)
Email overload	Collaborations involving many document updates may overload email	<	New versions posted directly to common repository

This solution is possible in Google Drive, which allows both PIM and GIM. However, Google Drive's design does not actively encourage folder categorization. In contrast, the typical Mac/ Windows interface encourages users to store their files in folders; if users attempt to close a file without categorizing it, then the system prompts them to do so. In Google Drive, files are stored automatically when they are created, and there is no point in time when the user is required to categorize them. If users want to categorize the file from within the editor, this can be done by selecting a folder icon, a feature that seems to be hard for many users to discover. Therefore, collaborators receiving a Google Drive link are not encouraged by the design to change the given categorization of the file (if there is one in the first place). We are currently developing cloud storage that allows for simultaneous editing on the one hand but encourages personal management of the file by each of the collaborators on the other. We will test whether this change will increase the percentage of files with meaningful names stored in folders and if such active organization in turn increases retrieval success and efficiency.

Another idea for future research relates to version management. In this study (Bergman, Whittaker, and Falk 2014), we asked participants to retrieve specific files, but collaborators usually create different versions of the same file, which were termed *versionsets* by Karlson, Smith, and Lee (2011). In such cases, it is important that collaborators retrieve the latest version of the file to avoid the possibility of ignoring new edits made by collaborators. Future research could compare PIM and GIM for retrieving the latest version of a versionset, using similar research methods and parameters as those we used here. In part III, we discuss *OldnGray*, a design that allows PIM users to identify most recent documents. This approach could be directly generalized to the GIM case, for which it also has important potential benefits.

Summary

Despite the increasing popularity of GIM methods for common cloud-based storage, our study (Bergman, Whittaker, and Falk 2014) documents some of their limitations. Although GIM boasts some intuitive benefits, people are less successful and less efficient at finding files in common repositories than in personal folders. Consistent with this, participants show a preference for more traditional methods of file sharing using email. Our data also suggest the reasons for better PIM retrieval: in PIM, people actively organize personal files by applying personal classifications that promote enhanced recall. Such active organization is less likely with GIM.

8 Why Is Navigation the Preferred PIM Retrieval Method?

The previous chapters in part II showed that folder hierarchies are the preferred method for PIM curation and retrieval, and that alternative methods such as search everything, tag everything, and group management are unlikely to replace them. This gives rise to a paradox: Despite the fact that these new technologies seem to offer intuitive benefits over folder navigation, users persist in using manual hierarchical curation and access via navigation. What, then, is the reason for the continued dominance of folders and navigation?

Bergman et al. (2008) offered the following speculations about possible reasons for preferring navigation over search:

Consistency: It is widely agreed that consistency is a virtue in design and human–computer interaction because it confirms user expectations (Shneiderman and Plaisant 2010). The hierarchical method is boringly consistent; files are stored in a "location" and stay there until users decide otherwise. Users therefore expect to find files in a particular place at retrieval. The process of navigation may require more steps than search, but users consistently follow those same steps. In contrast, the flexibility of search may compromise consistency, because users can retrieve the same file using different search terms. Even when using the same search term, results may be inconsistent, and the same file might appear in different places in the query results list at different times because of changes in the underlying search indexing algorithm. Consistency can also explain why users remember the locations of most of their retrieved files (chapter 5) and tend not to use multiple classifications (chapter 6). It is true that users *could* have stored files according to multiple categories, but after choosing a file and retrieving it from its location a few times, users seem to remember that it is there.

Recognition versus recall: As we noted in chapter 3, recognition memory tasks are easier and require less cognitive effort than recall tasks (Mandler 1980; Neisser 2014). When users perform a search, they typically have to generate a set of relevant search terms from scratch. The choice of terms is sometimes challenging, as it requires users to recall file names or attributes. In contrast, navigation is based mainly on recognition; each step down the hierarchy provides both incremental visual and contextual feedback about navigation success and concrete clues about the next choice of folder (Teevan et al. 2004; Jones 2013). Both search and navigation require that partial information be supplied by the user, but they differ in how users must provide that information (either immediately or over the course of an interaction) and how incremental feedback is supplied back to the user. It may therefore be the case that people's greater use of navigation represents a preference for a style of interaction based around specifying partial information incrementally and receiving iterative feedback each time additional information is provided.

Procedural versus declarative memory: Specifying a search term forces users to rely on declarative memory; that is, users have to know that the search term appears in a file. However, folder navigation can also rely on procedural memory—knowing how to navigate to a file (Barreau 1995). It also may be the case that users retain both "motor memory" and visual recognition about a file's location.

This chapter reports on two studies that provide complementary answers to the question of why navigation is preferred; both relate to underlying cognitive processes involved in navigation and search, but they use different methods to explore these processes. The *dual task study* hypothesizes that navigation is preferred because it requires less verbal cognitive attention than search. The *fMRI study* tests the same hypothesis and shows that search activates brain regions associated with verbal attention, which is a scarce resource that is typically in high demand for other tasks. In contrast, navigation involves "older" parts of the brain that have developed through millions years of evolution for navigation in the physical world and thus requires little verbal attention.

The Dual Task Study

One possible reason for navigation preference in PIM is that search requires more verbal attention. It is well-documented that humans have limited attentional capacity and that the mental processes necessary for many complex cognitive tasks compete for a limited set of resources (Treisman 1969). These demands are relevant to the retrieval situation, which calls for verbal attention. Search is not usually performed as an isolated task for its own sake. Instead, file retrieval is typically executed in the context of a primary task carried out before and after retrieval (e.g., a chemistry student whose primary task is writing a seminar paper retrieves a file called *Table of Elements* in order to complete the writing assignment). Therefore, it is reasonable to prefer a file retrieval method that requires less verbal attention. Reduced attention during retrieval allows users to keep their primary tasks in mind instead of having to switch attention to the retrieval process before attempting to resume and retrace their thinking. The main goal of our study (Bergman, Tene-Rubinstein, and Shalom 2013) was to test the hypothesis that navigation indeed requires less verbal attention than search. Before discussing our results, we will first provide background on the dual-task paradigm used in this experiment.

The Dual-Task Paradigm

The dual-task paradigm explores how people divide mental effort between two concurrent tasks. The concept of dual tasks can be demonstrated through the example of the chatty driver: Imagine an experienced driver who is driving while having a conversation with her passenger. Driving the car is the driver's *primary task*, and having a conversation is her *secondary task*. The fact that she can concentrate on the conversation indicates that she does not need to pay a lot of attention to the driving procedure itself; she can drive with a high degree of cognitive automation. Suddenly, she sees a child chasing a ball out into the road. At that moment, all of the driver's attention is focused on her driving; she pays no attention whatsoever to what her passenger is saying. Exploring performance across the two tasks allows us to determine where attention is allocated. At the moment the child ran into the road, the driver did not hear a word the passenger said (low performance on the secondary task), which indicates that all of her attention was needed for the primary task (driving).

The dual-task paradigm has been widely used in cognitive psychology for decades (Brown 1958; Peterson and Peterson 1959) and has been successfully applied to information science (Gwizdka 2010; Kim and Rieh 2005). Gwizdka (2010) asked his participants to perform a secondary task at different stages of a web search. He found that their performance on the secondary task was lower in the query formulation stage than in later stages of the search (scanning the search results and viewing individual web pages). This indicates that thinking of a search word is more cognitively demanding than performing later stages of the search process.

Baddeley (1992) found that there are two working memory components: verbal (the phonological loop) and visual (the visuospatial sketch pad). In our study (Bergman, Tene-Rubin-stein, and Shalom 2013), we chose a secondary task that was verbal, because in real life people are typically engaged in verbal tasks (such as writing a document or reading an email) before and after retrieval. We chose delayed free memory recall as the secondary task, a task widely used in cognitive psychology research.

The Recall Task

In the free recall task, participants are given a list of words and asked to recall as many words as they can in any order. In an immediate free recall task (i.e., when participants are asked to recall the words immediately after hearing them), participants tend to remember seven plus or minus two words (Miller 1956), although this can vary slightly depending on the language used.

In a delayed free recall task, participants hear the words and then either wait or do an unrelated intermediate task before being asked to recall them. When such delays or intermediate tasks are introduced, the number of words recalled decreases, with word recall negatively correlated with delay interval and the difficulty of the intermediate task (Brown 1958; Peterson and Peterson 1959). In order to keep the words in short-term memory during the intermediate task, participants need to use the phonological loop (a short-term memory component that keeps traces of words from decaying by rehearsing them); however, rehearsal is hard to execute when carrying out a concurrent demanding verbal task.

In our experiment, file retrieval was the intermediate task; participants were given a list of words, asked to retrieve a file, and then asked to recall as many words as they could. To successfully retrieve those words, participants needed to use the phonological loop to rehearse the words while retrieving the file. The more attention-demanding retrieval is, the less attention is available for the phonological loop and verbal rehearsal. The number of words remembered is therefore an indication of the amount of verbal attention required by the primary task. We used the number of words recalled in the secondary task to determine which retrieval method demands more attention—navigation or search.

Navigation Requires Less Verbal Attention than Search

Using a within-subjects design, our sixty-two participants remembered significantly more words in the free recall task when navigating to their target file than when searching for it. However, navigation retrievals were much faster than search retrievals, and time is known to have strong effect on the number of words remembered (Brown 1958; Peterson and Peterson 1959). Therefore, an alternative explanation for these results is that participants remembered more words after navigation than after search simply because navigation took less time than search. In order to eliminate this alternative explanation, we performed an analysis that controlled for retrieval time by including only the twenty-seven pairs of retrievals for which navigation time was similar to search time. A significant effect remained even when retrieval time was controlled. The fact that participants performed better on a secondary task when navigating than when searching indicates that navigation requires less verbal cognitive attention than search.

These results may explain the repeated strong preference for navigation over search that we described in chapter 5 and found in prior work (Barreau and Nardi 1995; Bergman et al. 2008; Boardman and Sasse 2004; Kirk et al. 2006; Teevan et al. 2004). Computer usage typically involves interleaved tasks that require users to retrieve information items in the service of a primary task—for example, retrieving a file while writing a document. Users therefore want to minimize the attentional demands of retrieval, making it possible for them to retain information about their primary task during retrieval. It is therefore rational to prefer the retrieval option that demands less attention— namely, navigation.

As we have observed in prior chapters, navigation may demand less attention because users are typically very familiar with their folder structures. Not only did they create their structures according to their own categorizations and subjective needs, but each time they navigate to their files they also become more familiar with their structures. Navigation therefore can be performed semiautomatically, leaving the mind free to think of other tasks at hand. Search, on the other hand, requires thinking of a search term, which has been shown to be an attention-demanding task (Gwizdka 2010). Moreover, there are several possible options to use in queries (e.g., different search terms), which may produce different result lists, and this such options do not contribute to familiarity.

Search Is Less Efficient than Navigation

Our results also showed that search took nearly three times longer than navigation; search is vulnerable to more mistakes and retrieval failures and is perceived to be more difficult in subjective evaluations. Some of these effects may be attributed to the fact that we did not allow our participants to type the target file name in the search box as it was given to them by the tester, but we did not put a similar constraint on navigation. However, participants indicated that this constraint made search only slightly more difficult than their usual searches. Therefore, we believe that these findings cast serious doubt on the assumption underlying the search everything approach: that search is more efficient and easier than navigation. Future research using other data-gathering techniques, such as search logs, could shed light on this question.

Another possible reason that navigation requires less attention than search is that virtual file navigation may rely on primitive brain structures that have evolved for physical navigation. Navigation may therefore exploit brain regions and processes that humans have evolved over millions of years to allow them to navigate in the physical world. Using these more primitive areas of the brain for retrieval may free other resource-limited parts of the brain to attend to more demanding tasks at hand.

Next, we will report on a study that tested this hypothesis by using fMRI.

The fMRI Study

In this study (Benn et al. 2015), we explored the neurocognitive bases of navigation and search in personal information management. We hypothesized that people prefer virtual folder navigation because of its similarities to real-world navigation. We predicted that the same brain structures involved in navigating physical environments would be employed in virtual navigation. These structures have been identified in animals (Bingman and Mench 1990; Furtak et al. 2007; Furuya et al. 2014) and humans (Epstein and Kanwisher 1998; Maguire, Frackowiak, and Frith 1997) and include regions of the posterior limbic system, such as the parahippocampal gyrus (Aguirre et al. 1996; Maguire, Frackowiak, and Frith 1996). In contrast, search competes for linguistic resources in working memory, as indicated by the results discussed in the previous section. Generating a search term is likely to engage cortical structures within the left fronto-temporal region, which are typically associated with linguistic and executive processing. We tested these neurocognitive hypotheses using functional magnetic resonance imaging (fMRI).

We collected whole-brain functional images from seventeen healthy, right-handed participants while they engaged in file retrieval using the standard Windows 7 operating system. To increase ecological validity, participants retrieved their own files from their personal laptops by following our EPIR procedure. Prior to the study, a list of recently used file names was extracted from each laptop. During the brain-scanning session, these file names were used as target items, and participants were asked to retrieve the target files from their laptops using either search or navigation as instructed. Two control tasks, one for search and one for navigation, were also included. The control tasks involved visual and motor activities matched to the search and navigation tasks but did not engage core cognitive processes involved in the experimental conditions (e.g., memory for virtual location or memory for file attributes).

Our results showed activation of different brain structures for search and navigation. As we expected, navigation resulted predominantly in bilateral activation of posterior regions of the brain, associated largely with real-world navigation, retrieving information from memory, and low-level sensory-perceptual processing. On the other hand, search resulted in strictly left-lateralized activation in areas strongly associated with linguistic and working memory processing (see figure 8.1).

These results, combined with those of the dual-task paradigm study (Bergman, Tene-Rubinstein, and Shalom 2013), provide a possible explanation for user preferences for navigation over search when retrieving items from digital personal collections. Virtual navigation for digital files involved bilateral activation of posterior brain regions, which are also engaged during navigation in the physical world (Epstein and Kanwisher 1998; Aguirre et al. 1996; Maguire, Frackowiak, and Frith 1996, 1997) and in which the level of theta activation (EEG of 4–8 hertz) has been shown to predict performance in navigating to a specific target (Cornwell et al. 2008). These same brain areas are also used for navigation by monkeys (Furuya et al. 2014), rats (see, e.g., Furtak et al. 2007), and pigeons (Bingman and Mench 1990). Combined with the observation that patients with severe

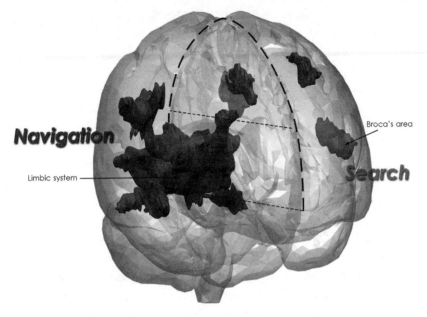

Figure 8.1

A 3-D model illustrating bilateral posterior region activation for folder navigation (darker gray) and left inferior frontal activation for search (lighter gray). The bold dotted line marks the external outline of the brain, and the two thin dotted lines mark the center line, dividing the left and right hemispheres. This figure was produced by creating a 3-D model of the standard brain via the 3D Slicer open access software (www .slicer.org). The 3-D activations were constructed and placed in the model using the information provided by each of the 2-D slices on the X, Y and Z planes. Figure created by Eran Apelbaum.

language difficulties following brain damage perform well on navigational tasks (Bek et al. 2010), it may be concluded that both virtual and real-world navigation requires little or no linguistic processing in the human brain.

Search, on the other hand, involved left-lateralized, mostly frontal activations that are associated with linguistic (Broca's area) and working memory processes (superior frontal gyrus; du Boisgueheneuc et al. 2006). These activations were not due to basic lexical retrieval, as our control task subtracted activations related to such processing. Instead, left inferior and superior frontal activations were likely to be linked to demands for linguistic-controlled processing such as attention and strategic planning, necessary for isolating precise search terms (Gwizdka 2010).

The need to actively generate a search term seems to divert linguistic and attentional resources to this task. These additional resource demands may explain why users choose to use search only as a last resort despite its flexibility. Activation of the left middle or superior frontal gyrus was also observed during navigation, suggesting that navigation also requires a degree of executive and working memory resources. However, these activations did not extend to linguistic structures, strengthening the argument that navigation requires minimal language mediation.

These findings offer a neurocognitive explanation for the repeatedly documented preference for navigation over search. They further explain why this preference has not altered despite advances in search engine technology and performance (see chapter 5) and imply that this navigation preference is unlikely to change with further improvements in search technologies. Throughout millions of years of evolution, humans have developed mechanisms that allow them to retrieve an item from a specific location (be it real or virtual) by navigating the path that they first followed when storing that information. These deep-rooted neurological biases lead to automatic activation of location-related routines, which have minimal reliance on linguistic processing, leaving the language system available for other tasks.

Part II: Summary

The first three chapters of part II explored various alternatives to hierarchical folder navigation and showed that search, tags, and group classification are unlikely to replace folder hierarchies for personal information management. The fourth chapter (chapter 8) provided cognitive and neurological explanations for this navigation preference. However, there are other technical alternatives that were not directly covered in these chapters, such automatic classification (discussed briefly in chapter 7) and the semantic desktop, which is the PIM equivalent of the semantic web. The semantic desktop applies machine learning methods to categorize a user's entire personal information collection (Ravasio et al. 2003; Adar, Karger, and Stein 1999; Karger and Quan 2004; Sauermann et al. 2006; Groza, Handschuh, and Moeller 2007; Woerndl and Woehrl 2008). Although it is perfectly legitimate to propose these or other new alternatives to folders, we reiterate the importance of testing whether such new approaches provide genuine improvements over navigation. For over three decades, scientists have been developing new systems that aim to replace folder hierarchies. However, the large majority of these proposed systems have not been evaluated empirically and none have been widely adopted by users, whereas folders are used almost exclusively for PIM curation by millions of users each day.

This raises an important question: why do methods that work so well outside PIM (such as web search and Web 2.0 tags) prove less useful in the PIM setting? We think that the key issue here is familiarity. Retrieval in the context of the web and Web 2.0 involves billions of documents, for which it is impossible to be familiar with their ever-changing structure. The model for interacting with such a structure necessarily involves search and information consumption. On the other hand, PIM involves far smaller document collections that users curate personally, as we discussed in part I. In PIM, the same user both organizes and retrieves information. Users are free to organize their information in a subjective way that suits their requirements. Users are therefore familiar with their own folder structures, which become even more familiar each time they navigate such structures. This familiarity helps users find their way to the files they seek. Furthermore, as we demonstrated in chapter 8, there are important cognitive reasons that navigation is preferred: Navigation is cognitively less demanding—unlike search, which requires complex verbal processing.

Part I and part II definitively demonstrate that personal information management is a different sort of game from other information management fields. Part III, the final part of the book, describes a design method developed specifically for PIM called the user-subjective approach to PIM systems design. This approach exploits the fact that the person who organizes information is the same person who retrieves it. In contrast to other proposed new methods, such as search, tags, and group information management, the user-subjective approach does not attempt to replace hierarchical folders. Instead, it exploits the unique characteristics of personal information management to incorporate new methods into an underlying hierarchical approach.

III   The User-Subjective Approach to PIM Systems Design

Part II of the book studied different PIM management and retrieval behaviors, showing that new technologies that attempt to replace navigation generally have not succeeded and providing explanations for this. However, those results do not address a critical PIM question—namely, how to design successful new systems. Curation research is not only about understanding how people keep, organize, and exploit their personal information; it is also about how we design new technologies that help people to be more successful in these processes. To address this design question, let's first recap what differentiates PIM curation from other forms of information management. We can use this understanding to motivate a set of design principles that provide guidelines for new PIM systems. We call these design principles the *user-subjective approach*. Our approach contrasts with prior attempts to design for information curation—such as those reviewed in part II—that have borrowed existing technologies from outside PIM. Instead, the principles and technologies we introduce here are developed explicitly for specific PIM requirements.

We have clearly shown that methods that work well in other fields (e.g., search for the web, tags for Web 2.0) are much less useful for curation. What is so unique about curation?

A fundamental difference between curation and other information-management fields (e.g., GIM or web access) relates to *familiarity*. As we saw in chapter 1, PIM is unique in that the person who curates the information is the same person who later retrieves it. The user-subjective design approach takes advantage of this unique feature and suggests that PIM systems should make systematic use of subjective (user-dependent) attributes.

The user-subjective approach is the first design approach developed specifically for PIM systems. In our first study (Bergman, Beyth-Marom, and Nachmias 2003), we first outlined the theory, and in our later study (Bergman, Beyth-Marom, and Nachmias 2008), we provided empirical support. Part III of the book extends that work by discussing further implementations and evaluations of PIM systems we have built to evaluate this approach. We have used this approach to design six implementations of different principles, and these implementations have been successfully deployed with positive user evaluations (Bergman et al. 2014; Bergman, Komninos, et al. 2012; Bergman et al. 2009; Kalnikaité and Whittaker 2007; Whittaker et al. 2004; Kalnikaité and Whittaker 2010).

In chapter 9, we introduce the user-subjective approach. Each of the following chapters (10–12) reports on one of its design principles: importance, project-based organization, and context. We describe user curation behaviors that motivate each principle and then demonstrate how each design principle is instantiated in specific implementations. User evaluations of several of these implementations provide strong evidence for individual principles and for the overall approach.

9   The User-Subjective Approach

In this chapter we will first recap why PIM is a different sort of game, then will introduce the concept of subjective attributes, which is central to the user-subjective approach, and finally present the three user-subjective principles.

Recap: The Communication Metaphor for the PIM Game

Recall the metaphor we used in chapter 1 to illustrate how PIM differs from other information management fields. Those other fields view the goal of information management as designing a communication channel between two people who have very different roles: an information professional (e.g., a website designer or a librarian) who organizes the information, and the user at the other end of the communication channel who finds and consumes it (see figure 9.1). Because information consumers differ from each other in multiple ways, the information professional is restricted to exploiting only public (i.e., user-independent) attributes when organizing information. PIM systems, in contrast, are unique in that the person who stores the information and decides on its organization is the same as

Figure 9.1
Traditional information management can be perceived as a communication channel between the information worker (left) and different information consumers (right).

the person who later retrieves it. Therefore, PIM can be seen as a special kind of solipsistic communication between a person and him- or herself during two different activities: storage and retrieval (see figure 9.2). The user-subjective approach exploits this unique feature, arguing that PIM systems should make systematic use of subjective, user-dependent attributes in addition to the traditional use of objective attributes. PIM systems should capture these subjective attributes when a user first interacts with an information item (either automatically or by using direct manipulation) in order to help the same user later retrieve that item.

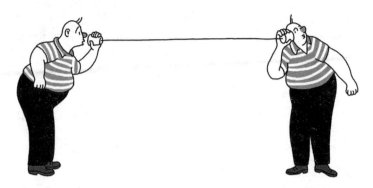

Figure 9.2
PIM can be perceived as communication between a person and him- or herself at two different time intervals.

Subjective Attributes

An early PIM study demonstrated the critical role of subjective attributes, inspiring the development of the user-subjective approach. Kwasnik (1991) analyzed the descriptions of eight faculty members who were asked to describe how they organize their personal documents. She found that a minority (30 percent) of the attributes described were document-related (e.g., author, form, topic, title). In contrast, the majority (70 percent) related to the interactions between the user and the information in the document, in particular how the user perceived and acted upon that information (e.g., situational attributes, disposition, time, cognitive state). Thus, users base their natural organization more on subjective attributes than on general public ones.

Attributes of an information item are labels that describe it and in doing so add value to it (Taylor 1986). We differentiate between public and subjective attributes. Public attributes are *user-independent*, in the sense that an external observer can infer these attributes directly from the information item without observing the user's actions. Such public attributes include the item's format, size, and date. In contrast, subjective attributes are *user-dependent* and cannot be derived directly from the information item itself. Instead, they often can be inferred from user–information interaction. For example, if a user frequently accesses a particular item, we might infer that item is subjectively important to that user.

The user-subjective approach identifies three specific subjective attributes: the *importance* of the information item to the user, the *project* to which it belongs, and the *context* in which the item is used. The approach suggests three design principles, one for each subjective attribute:

• The *subjective importance principle* states that the subjective importance of information should determine its degree of visual salience and accessibility.

• The *subjective project classification principle* states that information items that relate to the same subjective topic should be classified together regardless of their technological format or the application that generated them.

• The *subjective context principle* states that information should be retrieved and viewed by the user in the same context in which it was previously used.

These design principles are deliberately abstract to allow for multiple possible designs (as will be demonstrated in the instantiations of the importance and subjective context principles). In the remainder of part III, we define these three subjective attributes, propose a user-subjective design principle for each, and provide empirical support for each principle, derived from studies of deployed systems that implemented the design principle.

10   The Subjective Importance Principle

Importance is user-dependent and thus subjective: an information item can be very important to one person and completely unimportant to another. The same item might also be important and relevant to a user today but unimportant (irrelevant) to him or her next month. One measure of relevance can be derived from users' interactions with their information: Recently used information items are generally judged as more relevant than those that have not been used for a long time. We noted in part I that recent items are more likely to be retrieved than older items (Dumais et al. 2003; Fitchett and Cockburn 2015; Obendorf et al. 2007; Aula, Jhaveri, and Kaki 2005). The subjective importance principle states that information importance should determine the degree of visual salience and accessibility of an information item. We propose two complementary importance subprinciples: the *promotion* principle states that important information items should be highly visible and accessible, because they are more likely to be retrieved. The *demotion* principle proposes that information items of lower importance should be demoted (i.e., made less visible) so as not to distract the user, but should be kept within their original context just in case they are needed. Note that promotion

---

and demotion designs do not compete, because they address different needs. Keeping in mind that most information items are of medium importance, the promotion principle increases the salience and accessibility of highly important information items by separating them from the rest (normal and low importance). In contrast, the demotion principle downgrades information items of low importance by separating them from the rest (this time, those of normal and high importance; see figure 10.1).

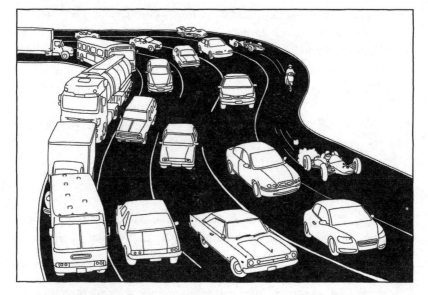

Figure 10.1
A highway metaphor for the difference between the promotion and demotion principles. Most vehicles are in the middle lane (items of medium importance), but there is a fast lane for fast vehicles (the promotion principle) and a slow lane for trucks that would otherwise slow down the middle lanes (the demotion principle).

Certain pervasive PIM designs are consistent with the promotion principle but predate the user-subjective approach; for example, PIM file systems have long allowed users to place important files on their desktops (making them visible and easy to access), following Malone (1983). Similarly, highly relevant items can be accessed by using recent document lists (at either the OS or application level). There are also experimental designs that are consistent with the promotion principle, such as Finder Highlights, which proactively highlights items that are likely to be accessed during navigation based on their access history (Fitchett, Cockburn, and Gutwin 2014). The demotion principle, in contrast, is a novel aspect of the user-subjective approach and has not been systematically explored before. Therefore, the remainder of this chapter will focus on demotion.

Demotion: An Intermediate Option between Keeping and Deleting

The keeping versus deleting decision was introduced in chapter 2, but in order to explain the concept of demotion, let's focus on the following question: Why is it critical to deal with information items of low importance? Jones (2004) claims that the decision about whether "to keep or not to keep" information for future usage is prone to two types of costly mistakes: On the one hand, information not kept is unavailable when it is needed later. On the other hand, irrelevant information items can create clutter if kept. Irrelevant items compete for a user's attention, obscuring important information relevant to the current task. It is well known in the field of cognitive psychology that in visual scanning, the number of irrelevant distracters increases the time taken for people to identify a target object (Neisser 1964;

Treisman and Gelade 1980). Thus, keeping irrelevant information not only causes guilt about being disorganized (Bellotti and Smith 2000; Whittaker and Hirschberg 2001), but also increases retrieval time. In addition, as we noted earlier, there is a deletion paradox: Unimportant information items distract attention and increase retrieval time for the target item, but it takes time and attention to review items in order to decide whether to keep or delete them (Bergman, Beyth-Marom, and Nachmias 2003). These are significant problems; millions of users curate and retrieve their personal information several times a day, and these problems will be exacerbated as personal collections continue to grow in size.

PIM studies repeatedly demonstrate that people experience problems in deciding what information to keep. Chapter 2 reviewed evidence from studies of paper, email, contact, photo, and web page collections. In general, except for web pages, people show a strong bias toward overkeeping information, sometimes of dubious value. People also show a tendency to defer keeping decisions until they have a clearer idea about the value of information. Some of the reasons for avoiding deletion are rational; a user can always think of a situation in which a particular information item may be needed (Whittaker and Hirschberg 2001). However, there are also psychological reasons that people avoid deletion, many of which can be attributed to the decision making process described in *Prospect Theory* (Kahneman and Tversky 1979):

• People judge losses and gains relative to a subjective reference point. There is an inherent asymmetry between the two decision alternatives. The decision to keep was already made when a file was first created or accepted. From then on, *to keep* is the default reference point, whereas *to delete* is a new, possibly risky alternative.

• People prefer alternatives that avoid a certain loss (even when the chance of incurring the loss is very small), and keeping avoids loss of an information item.

• Small objective probabilities are subjectively perceived as greater thus, the small probability that a deleted information item might be needed seems significant.

• Losses loom larger than gains; thus, the possible loss of an information item emotionally affects the decision maker more than the gains of having fewer distracters or reduced retrieval time.

To avoid these difficult deletion decisions, the demotion principle presents an intermediate option between *keep* and *delete*—offering the best of both worlds. Demotion allows information items of low importance to be made less visible without denying the user future access to those information items. This option combines both the advantage of the *delete* option (reducing competition for attention) and the advantage of *keeping* (allowing access to information if it is unexpectedly needed in the future). Finally, demotion supports deferral and short-circuits the difficult process of deciding whether or not to delete an item (Bergman, Beyth-Marom, and Nachmias 2003). Our results show that although demotion also requires a decision, it is easier for participants to make than the standard decision to delete, because the demotion decision involves lower risk (Bergman et al. 2009). In the past, deletion was a common strategy, not just to avoid distraction, but mainly to clear valuable hard disk memory space. Users had to choose between two main options: keep or delete. However, as memory storage has become larger and cheaper, storage space is less of a problem, and demotion is now a viable third option.

Motivation for the Subjective Importance Principle

Our motivations for each principle begin with an analysis of user behaviors to uncover problems with and work-arounds for existing technologies. In explorations of the subjective importance principle using multimethod research (Bergman, Beyth-Marom, and Nachmias 2008), we found that people understood and exploited promotional principles. Our participants used strategies that promoted important files (e.g., by placing them on the desktop), but because current systems offer no designated feature for demoting files, participants developed work-around strategies for demotion. For example, 40 percent of participants transferred some lower-importance items to an archive folder, 61 percent of participants moved them to an external memory store, such as a CD, 32 percent created a new folder for the same purpose and used the old one as an archive, and 24 percent of participants created an archive folder within the original folder. Altogether, 79 percent of participants used one or more of these alternatives to make at least some of their low subjective importance files less visible. The use of these workarounds to demote files confirmed the demotion principle and motivated our subsequent designs.

Implementation of the Demotion Principle

The user-subjective approach suggests that demotion interfaces need to keep information items within their original context. This is a critical point when comparing demotion with deletion or archiving (which can be either a user work-around or a design feature, as with email archiving in Microsoft Outlook and Gmail). In contrast to demotion, archiving removes the information item from its original context (e.g., the folder in which it was stored) to an archive folder. Preserving context is important, because—as we demonstrated in part II—people tend to retrieve information items from the location where they stored them. We will report on three demotion designs we have already evaluated: GrayArea, DMTR, and Old'nGray.

GrayArea

GrayArea allows users to demote files of low subjective importance by dragging them to a gray area at the bottom of the folder (see figure 10.2). As in all demotion interfaces, this process combines the advantage of deleting (unimportant files do not compete for attention) with the advantage of keeping (these files can be retrieved in the context of their original folders).

GrayArea's full design cycle was reported by Bergman et al. (2009); we first documented users' current work-around strategies, in which they demoted files as described earlier, then we tested three different paper prototypes for file demotion (GrayArea being one). We obtained feedback about the designs from seventy-nine participants. On the basis of that feedback, we decided on GrayArea and developed a working prototype for it. The last stage of the design cycle involved evaluating our prototype by asking ninety-six participants to carry out a common curation maintenance activity—that is, to "clean up" two of their folders under two conditions, once with GrayArea and once without it. Participants' logged actions in the two cleanup tasks are illustrated in figure 10.3.

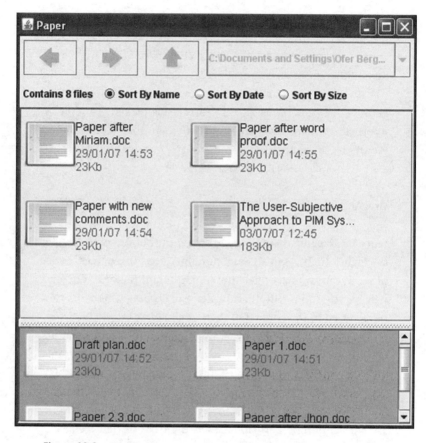

Figure 10.2
The GrayArea prototype. Demoted files appear at the bottom of the folder.

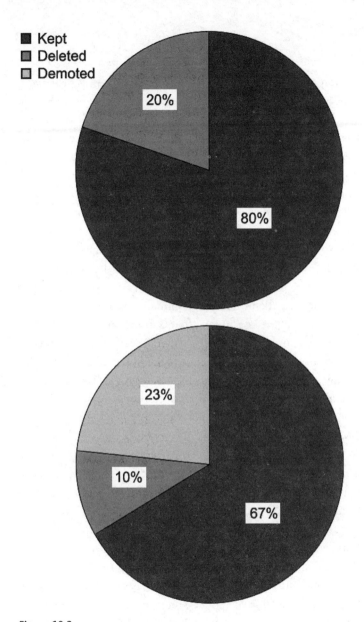

Figure 10.3
Average percentages of keeping, deleting, and demoting actions in the
standard condition (above) and in the GrayArea condition (below).

GrayArea reduced folder clutter by 13 percent; participants kept just 67 percent of files with GrayArea, compared to 80 percent with their standard operating system. Note also that the average deletion percentage dropped from 20 percent in the standard condition to 10 percent in the GrayArea one. Thus, we can view the 23 percent of demoted files in the GrayArea condition as comprising of 10 percent of files that might have been deleted in existing keep or delete interfaces (although, as we have noted, participants prefer not to delete), along with 13 percent of files that would have been kept (although participants would have preferred not to keep them). Further results show that 81 percent of participants found it easier to demote than delete files. The demotion decision may have been perceived as easier because it is less "final"; that is, users can always find the file in the context of the folder where it was stored and reverse the demotion by dragging the file to the upper part of the folder. Finally, most participants indicated they would use GrayArea if provided with the option in their operating systems.

DMTR

As we discussed in chapter 2, contact management is a critical aspect of PIM, and the standard strategy users employ is to overkeep contacts. One area in which this tendency is common is mobile phone management. Some contacts are frequently used (e.g., spouse and other "strong ties"), and others are used only occasionally ("weak ties"; Granovetter 1973). However, there is another group of contacts that have not been used for a long time and that users may doubt they will ever use again. Some of these unused contacts are people who were highly familiar in the past but who have lost their relevance, and others are contacts that have never been used (when bumping into an old school friend, taking each other's number can be an act of politeness rather than a practical matter). Just as unused files compete for the user's attention when retrieving a target file, unused contacts also distract, but here the mobile phone's limited display size makes unused contacts a critical problem.

To address this problem, we developed the *DMTR* prototype (Bergman, Komninos, et al. 2012). It shares several features in common with GrayArea. Like GrayArea, DMTR demotes unused contacts by presenting them at the bottom of the contact list in a smaller font, which (unlike regular contacts) is not bold (see figure 10.4). However, the demotion process works automatically rather than manually.

In the first phase of our study (Bergman, Komninos, et al. 2012), we asked eighteen participants to assess when they last used each of their mobile phone contacts. As we observed in Whittaker et al. (2002), many contacts were inactive: 47 percent had not been used for over six months or had never been used. In the second phase, we demoted these unused contacts via DMTR. After two months, we asked our participants to locate contacts that they had recently used, with and without the prototype. Results indicate that the use of DMTR reduced both the number of key strokes and the retrieval time significantly when accessing those contacts. The majority of participants also indicated that it was easier to access their contacts using DMTR and that they would like to use DMTR on their next mobile phone.

Old'nGray

One problem mentioned repeatedly by participants in PIM studies (e.g., Bergman 2006; Boardman 2004) arises from the fact

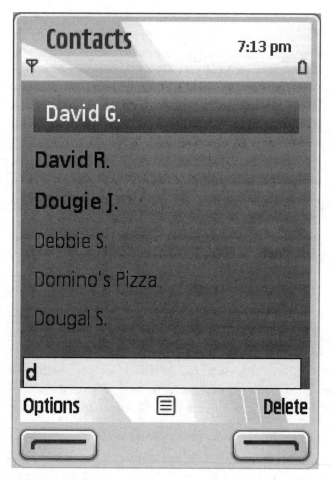

Figure 10.4
DMTR interface.

that users keep multiple versions of the same file. These versions are typically improved sequentially over time, so in the large majority of cases, users are interested in retrieving only the latest version. When seeking this latest version, users may become confused and distracted by previous versions of the file. The presence of prior versions can negatively affect retrieval and potentially lead to wasted effort in editing and reconciling prior versions. We term the effort involved in finding the correct, most recent file the *recent version problem*. *Old'nGray* is a working prototype that addresses the recent version problem by automatically identifying the most recent version of the file and then graying out the file icons of older versions of files (Bergman et al. 2014). This design aims to help users ignore older versions of the file, enabling them to spot the latest version at a glance by using perceptual rather than cognitive processes (see figure 10.5). Although standard file browsers allow users to sort files by date, the performance of Old'nGray is more successful and efficient than simple chronological sorting.

The prototype also provides other options that are triggered by right-clicking on the older versions of the file: (a) opening the latest version of the file even if it is in another folder (or even an email attachment); (b) displaying and accessing all versions of the file, even if they are scattered across the user's computer; and (c) reversing the graying action for a version of particular importance to the user.

We tested our prototype using a within-subjects design ($N = 60$), in which participants were asked to locate the most recent version of a particular file. Use of Old'nGray drastically reduced file access failures from an average of 24 percent in the control condition to 4 percent. It also reduced retrieval time from an average of 17.68 seconds in the control condition to 6.56

Organize ▾	Include in library ▾	Share with ▾	Burn	New folder		
Name			Date modified	Type		Size
Old'nGray core 1.0.docx			04/08/2013 00:...	Microsoft Word ...		14 KB
Old'nGray for review.docx			04/08/2013 08:...	Microsoft Word ...		14 KB
Old'nGray paper 1.2.docx			04/08/2013 02:...	Microsoft Word ...		14 KB
Paper on Old'nGray – definitely final 2.do...			12/08/2013 01:...	Microsoft Word ...		14 KB
Paper on Old'nGray – definitely final.docx			11/08/2013 09:...	Microsoft Word ...		14 KB
Paper on Old'nGray – final final.docx			10/08/2013 12:...	Microsoft Word ...		14 KB
Paper on Old'nGray - final.docx			04/08/2013 10:...	Microsoft Word ...		14 KB
paper proposal – including images.docx			03/08/2013 19:...	Microsoft Word ...		14 KB
paper proposal – new version.docx			03/08/2013 18:...	Microsoft Word ...		14 KB
paper proposal.docx			03/08/2013 17:...	Microsoft Word ...		14 KB
remarks for proposal.docx			03/08/2013 19:...	Microsoft Word ...		14 KB

Figure 10.5
The effect of the Old'nGray prototype on folder presentation. Icons of all previous versions of the files are grayed out, allowing users to identify the latest version at a glance.

seconds with Old'nGray. As we expected, the benefits of Old'nGray increased with folder size. People used chronological sorting in only half of the control condition retrievals, which may explain the high failure percentage. The use of chronological sorting also resulted in additional retrieval time compared to the use of Old'nGray. Seventy percent of participants indicated that they would like the prototype to be integrated into their next operating system.

Demotion and Search
The use of demotion principles implemented in GrayArea and Old'nGray is not limited to retrieval from folders; it can also be

applied to retrieval using search. Currently, search results often include information items of low subjective importance. For example, considerable time may be spent in distinguishing the latest version of a document from older ones stored in other folders (e.g., an archive folder), because queries typically search across folders (Jones, Karger, et al. 2005). One design suggestion that applies demotion to search is to distinguish the information items marked in GrayArea and Old'nGray from the rest of the results in the list when a user searches by way of their gray color (see figure 10.6), allowing users to identify the most recent non-demoted versions more easily.

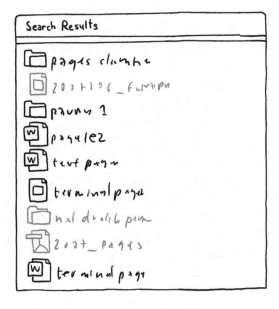

Figure 10.6
Demoted search results are faded to reduce their salience.

Summary

The subjective importance principle states that importance should determine the visual salience and accessibility of information. It is divided into two subprinciples: The promotion principle proposes that important items should be highly visible and accessible because they are more likely to be retrieved, and the demotion principle proposes that items of lower importance should be made less visible so as not to distract the user, but kept in their original context. Our initial explorations of the subjective importance principle indicated that participants tended to use existing interface designs to promote important files (e.g., by placing them on the desktop). However, because current systems offer no designated feature for demoting files, participants found their own work-arounds for demotion. These observations, combined with the fact that users' collections are cluttered with unimportant information items (Abrams, Baecker, and Chignell 1998; Boardman and Sasse 2004; Jones 2004; Kirk et al. 2006; Whittaker and Sidner 1996), motivated the development of three different user-subjective designs for demotion: GrayArea, DMTR, and Old'nGray. All three were shown to be effective in empirical evaluations. Note the deliberately abstract form of the design principle; for example, we deliberately didn't specify the mechanism by which demotion should occur. This allows for other designs that comply with the principle that might involve an item being demoted automatically by the software or manually by the user. Nor does the principle state how demoted items should be depicted to make them less salient. Stating principles abstractly is critical in promoting multiple potential designs and in allowing designs to be generative. The positive evaluation of the three prototypes validates the demotion principle and the user-subjective approach as a whole. We are currently in the development stage of another demotion interface, called *DupliPix*, which partially hides near duplicates of pictures, and we expect more demotion interfaces to be generated and evaluated in the future.

11   The Subjective Project Classification Principle

Information items seldom exist in isolation. Usually, when we work on a document or presentation, we need to discuss it over email with collaborators, maybe basing its contents on data from a website that we have bookmarked. It is imperative when working on each information item that such related materials are easily retrieved and viewed together (Dumais et al. 2003). It has been repeatedly observed that users experience problems in integrating information that relates to a common project, because that information is scattered across different applications or folders (Balakrishnan, Matthews, and Moran 2010; Yarosh et al. 2009; Bergman, Beyth-Marom, and Nachmias 2006; Kaptelinin 2003). Take Jane, for example, a chemistry student who has a Chemistry folder in each of three format-dependent hierarchies (documents, emails, and favorites). Her chemistry project is fragmented between these three collections. When she works on chemistry, she needs to navigate among these separate folders, and doing so can be quite onerous (see figure 11.1). We describe this problematic situation as *the project fragmentation problem* (Bergman, Beyth-Marom, and Nachmias 2006). Project fragmentation occurs when a user who is working on a single project stores information items relating to that project in

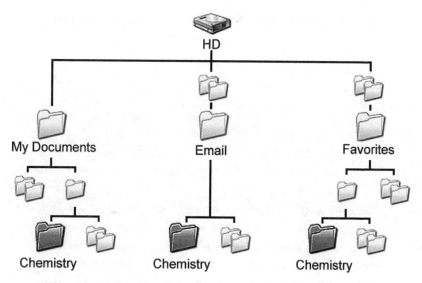

Figure 11.1
Example of the project fragmentation problem. Information related to the same chemistry course is fragmented into separate collections, making it difficult to retrieve related items together.

separate, format-related collections from which he or she also retrieves them.

The *subjective project classification principle* addresses this problem, specifying PIM designs that allow users to straightforwardly store related information items together regardless of application or format. Other work observes that items in PIM are often classified under the projects[1] that the users are involved in (Jones, Phuwanartnurak, et al. 2005). *Project* is a subjective attribute of an information item chosen by the PIM user, and thus the same information item might be classified under different projects for different users. For example, a person attending a conference might classify the URL of the conference hotel in a folder with the conference name within her web favorites, but the same URL could be placed in a Honeymoon folder by a future bride planning to visit the hotel for during her honeymoon.

The subjective project classification principle states that designs should allow all information items related to the same project to be classified under the same category regardless of their technological format. Although project-based classification has been encouraged in experimental systems (Bellotti and Smith 2000; Dourish et al. 1999; Freeman and Gelernter 1996; Jones, Munat, and Bruce 2005; Kaptelinin 2003; Karger and Quan 2004; Boardman 2004), current PIM system designs discourage such classification (Boardman, Spence, and Sasse 2003). Instead, current systems encourage users to classify their information items according to projects—but within their format-related hierarchy. The result is fragmentation: documents relating to a given project are stored in one folder hierarchy (e.g., in My Documents), emails in a separate mailbox hierarchy, and favorite websites in yet another browser-related hierarchy (these will be referred to as the *three hierarchies*). The only exception to this fragmentation problem in current PIM systems design is in the case of documents, in which all different formats of documents (e.g., Word, Excel, and PowerPoint documents) can be classified in the same file hierarchy.

Motivation for the Subjective Project Classification Principle

Observations of user behaviors provide motivation for the project principle. Bergman, Beyth-Marom, and Nachmias (2006, 2008) explored the use of the project attribute in current PIM systems. We found that personal computer users tend to refer to their information items according to the project the items are associated with rather than in terms of their formats. Although users often concurrently use different information-item formats (documents, email, and web favorites) while working on a project, they nevertheless usually save these items into the three separate, format-related hierarchies. Occasionally, the folders in which those common items are stored (in the different hierarchies) are named consistently according to the relevant project (Boardman, Spence, and Sasse 2003; Jones, Karger, et al. 2005). However, consistent naming by project is the exception and not the rule. Bergman, Beyth-Marom, and Nachmias (2006) also found that when the interface design encourages it, personal computer users will store project-related information items of different formats in one project folder and retrieve them together from that location. However, when the design does not encourage it, users store project-related information items in the three hierarchies.

Implementation of the Subjective Project Classification Principle

To address project fragmentation and to implement the subjective project classification design principle, we propose the *single hierarchy solution*, in which all project-related information items are stored in the same folder regardless of format (Bergman, Beyth-Marom, and Nachmias 2006) by combining the three hierarchies into a single folder hierarchy. One possible implementation of the single hierarchy solution is Project-Folders, which has been designed but not yet implemented or evaluated.

The ProjectFolders system design is an instantiation of the project classification principle. It allows a user to store all project-related documents, emails, and web favorites as well as related tasks and contacts in a single folder, separated by tabs. This allows users to work in the context of their projects and retrieve all project-related items from a single location. Figure 11.2 shows a concept illustration of ProjectFolders as envisioned when users open a folder via Finder or Windows Explorer. When opening an application, only related information items will be presented (emails for the mailbox and favorite websites for the browser). Note that this solution does not require or even advise

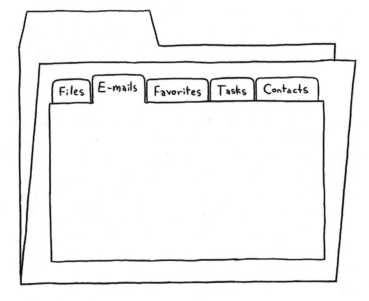

Figure 11.2
The ProjectFolders scheme. Related items are presented together regardless of their application or format.

the unification of different PIM applications, only their default storage locations.

We are not alone in addressing this problem, and we will now review prior solutions. Early attempts to address project fragmentation can be divided into two categories: integration through search and integration through an additional structure distinct from existing format-dependent hierarchies.

Integration through search: Several search tools address the project fragmentation problem by enabling users to search for items related to the same project in the context of a single query, regardless of format. Such tools include SIS (Dumais et al. 2003), Lifestreams (Fertig, Freeman, and Gelernter 1996b), and Presto (Dourish et al. 1999). Query results are presented in a single context, allowing a user to see all documents within a project. This approach is now implemented in both Mac OS X and Windows search engines. The ability to search across multiple formats is certainly a positive feature of search tools, but the effect on the fragmentation problem might be limited. As we indicated in chapter 5, users prefer navigation to search and use search only as a last resort. Another limitation of the search approach relates to the accuracy of desktop search, which often returns items that are only tenuously related to the original query. Such marginally related items may compromise the benefits of project-based search by introducing irrelevant or distracting content.

Integration through additional structure: Additional structure tools allow a user to create projects in an additional structure distinct from the three hierarchies. Several experimental systems employ this strategy, such as Raton Laveur (Bellotti and Smith 2000), UMEA (Kaptelinin 2003), TaskTracer (Dragunov et al. 2005), and SWISH (Oliver et al. 2006), as well as commercial software such as OneNote, Snippets, and DragStrip. Although the additional structure solution allows users to work in an integrated project environment, it requires managing yet another structure and may increase cognitive complexity. As well as the additional requirement to create a new structure, the user now has yet another retrieval location to maintain and remember.[2]

Integrated search and additional structure approaches both assume that project fragmentation is inevitable. In contrast, ProjectFolders addresses the problem by avoiding fragmentation in the first place. Some may consider ProjectFolders a radical solution because it unites information items of different applications (file browser, email, and web browser). Moreover, it requires users to change their storage habits. However, interface design often dictates users' preferences and strategies, so changing the interface may change user behavior and improve usability (Shneiderman and Plaisant 2010). For example, in the early 1990s, each document application suggested a separate storage location; for example, WordStar documents were stored in a separate location from Lotus Notes files, and Photoshop files were in yet another place. This led users to follow these defaults by storing application files in different locations. However, now that current systems offer a single storage location for all documents (e.g., My Documents), users tend to store project-related documents of different formats in the same folders, as indicated by our data (Bergman, Beyth-Marom, and Nachmias 2006). Thus, the ProjectFolders design may lead to a similar change for all project-related information items.

Summary

Our data show that users tend to think about their information items in terms of projects. They simultaneously retrieve information items of different formats when working on the same project and store files of different formats together according to projects when the system design allows them to. However, current system designs discourage users from storing emails and web favorites with files, so people currently store these items in separate folder hierarchies. Following the subjective project principle, we address project fragmentation by proposing a single hierarchy solution in which all project-related information items are stored in the same folder hierarchy regardless of format, so files, emails, web favorites, tasks, and contacts are stored together and separated by tabs. In future research, we hope to develop ProjectFolders to evaluate the single hierarchy solution.

12 The Subjective Context Principle

When users interact with their personal information, they do so in a certain context—but when the interaction ends and the user and information item each go their separate ways, the context of the interaction is lost, unless it is deliberately preserved by the system. Much prior research has suggested that users experience considerable difficulties regenerating that prior context when time has elapsed (Czerwinski, Horvitz, and Wilhite 2004; González and Mark 2004; Whittaker et al. 1997). The *subjective context principle* suggests that information should be retrieved by the user in the same context in which it was previously used in order to bridge the time gap between retrieval and prior use.[1]

Motivation for the Subjective Context Principle

As in previous cases, our design principle is motivated by empirical observations of user behaviors. For example, a common process in PIM involves users distilling complex information into a summary that is to be used at a future time. Typical examples might include taking notes in a meeting or summarizing a lecture or presentation. One frequently encountered difficulty in such situations is that these notes can be difficult to understand later because their original context is forgotten. Our early empirical work showed that participants experienced problems after a meeting interpreting notes taken during the meeting because notes were often too cryptic for current information needs (Whittaker et al. 2008). More specifically, users complained about being unable to understand meeting summary notes that included complex technical descriptions or acronyms because initial notes were too cursory (Whittaker et al. 2008; Kalnikaité and Whittaker 2010). What users wanted was to be able to straightforwardly reconstruct that original meeting context in order to interpret their prior summaries.

The user-subjective approach identifies four context attributes of an information item: internal, external, social, and temporal. *Internal context* relates to the user's thoughts while interacting with the information item; the *external context* of an information item refers to the other items that the user was dealing with while interacting with a specific information item; *social context* refers to other persons relating to the information item, such as other people who collaborate with the user regarding that information item; and *temporal context* pertains to the state in which the user left the information item when she or he last interacted with it and to his or her working plans regarding that information.

A content analysis of interviews in which participants talk about their personal information while showing the tester how they manage it (a PIM research technique called the *guided tour*; see chapter 4) reveals that half of the participants' utterances referred to at least one of these contextual attributes (Bergman, Beyth-Marom, and Nachmias 2008). Although the notion that information should be understood in its context is widely accepted in the field of information science (Medlin and Schaffer 1978; Saracevic 1999; Schamber 1994) and in the specific field of PIM research (Barreau 1995; Kwasnik 1991; Malone 1983), current PIM systems typically fail to keep context even in simple cases, such as linking between an attachment and the email it was delivered in, allowing a user to annotate a file, or providing easy ways to indicate the temporal state in which a user left an item during the work process.

Implementation of the Subjective Context Principle

The following sections present five examples of implementations of the context principle for each of the four context attributes. Three implementations have been evaluated so far.

ChittyChatty (Internal Context)

We have described how meeting and lecture participants experience problems in interpreting summary notes without prior context. We therefore built a system *ChittyChatty* that allows users to reconstruct relevant parts of their original context by linking notes to recordings of that context. The system uses a method we call cotemporal indexing. The system records user notes along with a recording of the original meeting or lecture. These user notes are synchronized with the underlying meeting recording (see figure 12.1, which shows the *ChittyChatty* system). Clicking on a given note allows students or meeting participants to return to the exact time in the lecture or meeting when the note was taken, and the system begins replaying what was said in the lecture at that time. Users can reconstruct the original context by listening to the recording. For example, clicking on the "Attend Information Retrieval Lecture on 7th

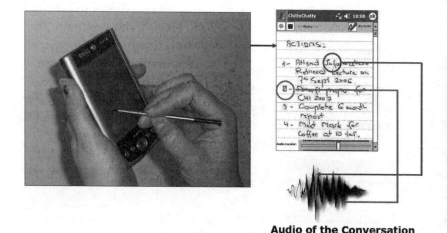

Audio of the Conversation

Figure 12.1
ChittyChatty UI for retrieving lecture context for handwritten notes. The system records user notes along with speech from the original meeting and coindexes them. Clicking on a digital note accesses the original speech that occurred when the note was taken, allowing context to be regenerated.

September 2006" note prompts the system to replay what was said when that note was taken so that the user can listen again to the original conversation describing exactly why this action was committed to.

We have built and evaluated multiple implementations of this approach that provide strong supporting evidence for the subjective context principle. Variants of *ChittyChatty* were evaluated both in a long-term field study and in lab settings. A two-year naturalistic class deployment demonstrated that having the system available when taking notes and during retrieval improved student grades because it allowed students to better understand their class notes. Students who accessed the system more frequently obtained better grades. A second controlled evaluation showed that students using the system outperformed those using traditional handwritten notes or handouts to answer class quizzes (Kalnikaité and Whittaker 2010). Earlier evaluations provide evidence from deployments and lab evaluations that similar designs improved understanding of meeting notes (Whittaker, Hyland, and Wiley 1994) and memory of personal conversations (Kalnikaité and Whittaker 2007). A similar design was effective for digital educational videos (Bergman et al. 2000; Dekel and Bergman 2000).

ItemHistory (External Context)

In his 1945 article "As We Might Think," Bush envisioned a machine he termed *Memex*, which automatically indexed information items sequentially viewed by users in associative trails in order to allow users to return to these information items in the future. Seventy years after the article was written, current PIM systems still do not allow a user to follow a trail from one information item to another when the two are viewed at approximately the same time. Implementing the subjective context principle, *ItemHistory* is a feature that provides this functionality. When working on a specific information item (e.g., a student working on a course paper), a user may open several other information items related to the same task (e.g., web pages, emails, and other documents containing relevant information). In current designs, the connections between these information items are lost and the user needs to retrieve each of them separately. ItemHistory indexes these relations automatically. When the need arises, a user can use this feature

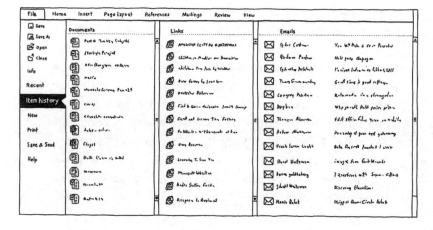

Figure 12.2
ItemHistory design scheme. The user interface shows documents, web pages, and emails that were concurrently open at a given time.

(e.g., as an additional option listed in the item's File menu) to view and retrieve all items that were open at the same time as the current one (see figure 12.2). Similar work on personal information history has been conducted by Hill and Hollan (1994), Hill et al. (1992), and Ringel et al. (2003).

ContactMap and PiccyChatty (Social Context)

ContactMap categorizes personal information according to its social context (Whittaker et al. 2004; Nardi et al. 2002). A common way for users to retrieve personal information is in terms of the person or social group that shared that information. Email retrievals often involve specifying a sender (Elsweiler 2008; Whittaker et al. 2011), and folder labels sometimes describe individuals or groups the user is actively working with. Our initial interviews revealed that users commonly relied on social attributes for organization and retrieval (Whittaker et al. 2004). ContactMap explicitly recognizes these social relations, allowing users to access information based on the people and groups that either created or shared that information. We first identified groups of important social contacts by analyzing a user's email interactions with those people, selecting contacts the user emailed both often and in the long term (Whittaker et al. 2002). We also were able to infer relations between groups of contacts by seeing which contacts co-occurred in the *to* and *from* fields. These groups were used to organize desktop information such as documents or emails (see figure 12.3, in which spatial clustering, group icons and color coding all signal relations among groups of contacts). By clicking on a group, users can retrieve the set of emails exchanged between those contacts or the sets of documents they have exchanged via email attachments. The system also supports social reminding by signaling actionable items (such as unread emails) associated with each group or contact. ContactMap was compared with a regular email client in a series of lab tests and field deployments, outperforming that client on four different socially oriented work communication tasks—for example, retrieving emails associated with an active collaborative project.

Social information also can be highly useful in GIM contexts. Frequency of access is known to be an indicator of the importance of an information item (Fitchett and Cockburn 2015; Whittaker et al. 2002). *PiccyChatty* used social information to infer the relative importance of information items shared with others (Kalnikaité and Whittaker 2008b). It was again deployed in an educational context, allowing users to take notes when learning complex verbal materials during lectures. *PiccyChatty*, users could actively annotate important parts of the lecture, but

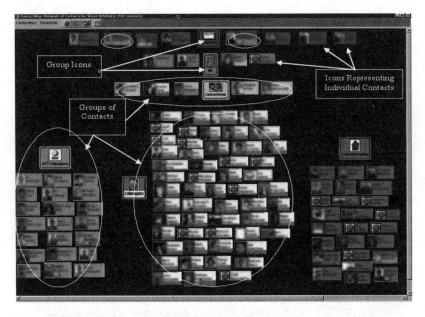

Figure 12.3
ContactMap user interface, showing social organization of personal information into distinct groups of associated contacts along with their underlying information. Clicking on an individual contact or group of contacts retrieves all emails involving those contacts. Icons representing individual contacts are blurred to preserve anonymity.

the system also allowed users to take photos, which could, for example, capture an important slide that the lecturer presented. As with the *ChittyChatty* system described earlier in this chapter, notes or photos were temporally coindexed to lecture recordings to allow recreation of initial context so that clicking on a note or photo would begin playback of what was being said when the note or photo was created.

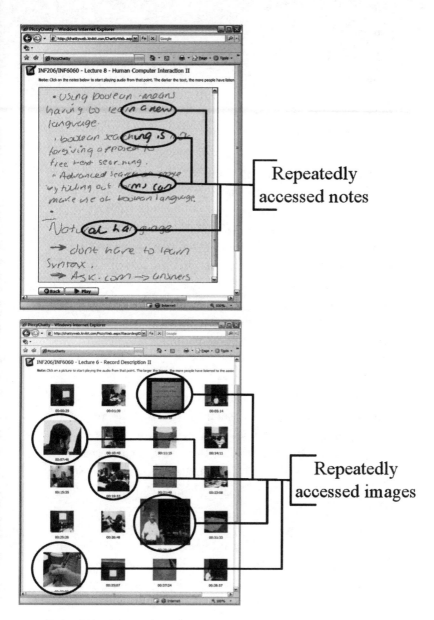

Figure 12.4
Social information signals salient parts of a lecture recording in *PiccyChatty*. Larger photos or bolded notes are those accessed by more participants, suggesting more important parts of the lecture.

In *PiccyChatty*, notes and photo annotations were pooled across all system users, and the system recorded social information about how many people had accessed a specific note or photo. This social frequency information was then incorporated into the user interface to increase the salience of frequently accessed items and decrease the salience of less frequently accessed items. Figure 12.4 shows the two versions of the interface for notes and photos; larger photos or bolded notes indicate items that have been accessed by many people. Evaluation of the system showed that social information was beneficial for both notes and photos: versions of the system that included social information improved user performance over versions that omitted social information. In a long-term deployment, students using the social version had higher class grades than those who used non-social-system versions.

Starlight (Temporal Context)

In part I of the book, we described how actionable items are pushed out of sight in the email inbox and consequentially forgotten. Many users may mark such messages as important (e.g., using a star in Gmail), but unless they are using a special inbox mode (e.g., "starred first" in Gmail), these messages may still be pushed out of sight—and also out of mind. Our Starlight design gives users continuous reminders about their actionable items within a chronological presentation by presenting the number of messages marked as important visually. It does so by presenting a star (or a similar icon) for each important message at the top of the email screen. Figure 12.5 illustrates Starlight within the Gmail interface, although a similar interface can be designed for other email applications. Users can see at a glance how many actionable messages they still have to attend to. Hovering

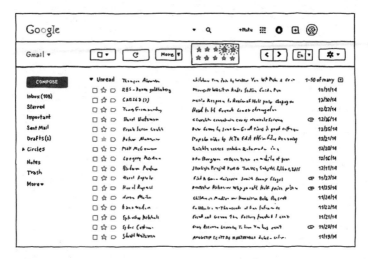

Figure 12.5
Starlight scheme. An array of stars above the message list shows that a user has ten starred items (even though only one of these is currently visible). The two shining stars indicate impending deadlines.

above each star shows the name of the message, and clicking it retrieves the message. By using semantic algorithms that analyze important messages, Starlight will also detect due dates (e.g., a conference date or "next Tuesday") and alert the user by making each star "shine" increasingly brightly as its deadline approaches.

Part III: Summary

In the previous parts of the book, we argued that PIM is a different sort of game from other information management fields. In this part, we focused on the ways that new designs might help users play this game more effectively. We introduced the user-subjective design approach and its three principles, demonstrating the use of subjective attributes with nine design schemes. In most cases, we presented system deployments and their evaluations as evidence for the effectiveness of both the specific design and the user-subjective design principles more generally. Support for the approach is twofold: First, our initial research (Bergman, Beyth-Marom, and Nachmias 2008) indicates that current PIM system users engage in work-arounds in which they seek to exploit subjective attributes in their natural PIM practices. Second, our follow-up system implementations show positive user evaluations of six different designs derived from these user-subjective principles (Bergman et al. 2014; Bergman, Komninos, et al. 2012; Bergman et al. 2009; Kalnikaité and Whittaker 2007; Whittaker et al. 2004; Kalnikaité and Whittaker 2010). We conclude part III by discussing three key issues.

Unlike the search everything and tag everything approaches, the user-subjective approach does not attempt to replace the hierarchical method. Instead, it takes folders as a given and attempts to improve the hierarchical method by uniting different folder hierarchies (e.g., ProjectFolders) and adding features to folders (e.g., GrayArea). However, the user-subjective approach does not take a stance in the argument between hierarchical design and the various alternatives we talked about in part II. This is because any PIM design might benefit from systematic exploitation of subjective attributes (as demonstrated in the demotion and search section of chapter 10).

We deliberately did not attempt to patent any of our design applications because we want users of all operating systems to benefit from them. It is our hope that the next generation of Windows, Mac, Linux, and Chrome operating systems will include user-subjective designs such as GrayArea and Old'nGray and that mobile phones will include features such as DMTR.

Most importantly, the user-subjective approach is a *generative* approach. When first proposing our principles (Bergman, Beyth-Marom, and Nachmias 2003), we did not have a clear vision of the ways in which they would be implemented. Later, using our abstract design principles, we created several demonstrably useful designs. These may look straightforward, but they were motivated by the principles and did not exist prior to our approach. We hope that in the future, PIM system designers will use the user-subjective approach to assist curation and implement its principles in unexpected ways that have not occurred to us.

Conclusions and Future Directions

We conclude with a brief summary of each chapter, outlining major points made along the way. We end the book by focusing on the future, proposing outstanding questions regarding new curation theory, research, and technology.

Book Summary

Part I argued that information science has focused almost exclusively on seeking and consuming new public information. It has overlooked the importance of personal information and critical research questions about how people curate and manage their personal archives. Part I began by describing key differences between the curation and consumption models. It defined *personal information*, outlined the critical curation processes of keeping, management, and exploitation, and reviewed prior research about each process.

Chapter 1 made the case for curation and described its constituent processes. It critiqued existing models of information consumption and established the importance of personal archives. It characterized the properties of different types of information and the effects of these properties on curation activities.

Chapter 2 described keeping. People don't keep personal copies of every information item that they encounter, so they have to actively decide what to keep. We reviewed evidence showing that keeping is cognitively challenging because it requires people to predict future information needs. These cognitive difficulties lead people to *overkeep*, retaining low-value information that in many cases they never access, which potentially interferes with their retrieval of valuable information.

Chapter 3 described how we manage our information to anticipate future information needs. The chapter drew distinctions between informative and actionable items. *Actionable items* require special treatment; they must be reaccessed at a specific time. We discussed why management is difficult: Users have to predict how they will be thinking about their information at the time of retrieval. We described different strategies for management, along with their costs and benefits. We contrasted *filing*, in which a user organizes information into folders based on systematic semantic classification, with *piling*, which is a more laissez-faire strategy that organizes information into simple categories, often based on the time that they were received.

Chapter 4 discussed *exploitation*—how we retrieve the information that we have kept and managed. We reviewed different access strategies, contrasting folder navigation with search. We described regularities in retrieval, including a bias for recent information.

Part II documented how and why navigation is the dominant PIM retrieval strategy. We described multiple studies that compare navigation with alternative retrieval methods. Those alternative methods have worked well in other information management domains, including search on the web and tags for Web 2.0. However, they do not generalize well to PIM. We reviewed multiple studies showing an overall preference for navigation and argued that there are important cognitive reasons for this preference. Navigation requires that users actively categorize their information as they create folders; this active categorization is crucial for retrieval. Further studies provide supporting cognitive and neurological explanations for navigation preference.

Chapter 5 examined different retrieval strategies for accessing personal information. It documented a clear preference for navigation over search. We described a study that used multiple methods to show that this preference is independent of the quality of the search engine used. Unlike finding new information on the web, which requires search, people use search only as a last resort when accessing personal files.

Chapter 6 demonstrated that tags, which work so well for Web 2.0, show low adoption rates when curating personal data; people prefer folders over tags, and even when using tags, they rarely use more than a single tag per information item.

Chapter 7 addressed group information management. We showed that file retrievals from folders that are shared and co-organized in the cloud are less successful than retrievals of files received via email attachments and stored in PIM folders.

Chapter 8 explored fundamental reasons for navigation preferences. We used methods from cognitive science and neuroscience to explain why navigation is preferred over search. These methods indicate that navigation is less cognitively demanding than search.

Part III built on the results from part II, proposing new system design principles that specifically target PIM. Part II documented the failure of efforts to exploit techniques from other areas of information science for curation; part III therefore proposes the user-subjective design approach, which is the first to address the specific requirements of curation. This approach exploits the fact that PIM is a different sort of game by incorporating subjective design attributes into PIM systems. We proposed specific design principles: importance, project-based organization, and context. We presented exemplar systems that implement each principle, along with several evaluations of their deployment.

Chapter 9 elaborated upon a communication metaphor for PIM, viewing PIM as a solipsistic conversation between a person at the time of storage and the same person at time of retrieval. We use this metaphor to explain why PIM systems are unique, arguing that they can (and should) support the use of subjective attributes.

Chapter 10 focused on the *demotion principle*, which advocates that unimportant information items should be made less salient in order not to distract the user but kept in their original context in case they are needed. We presented three designs that were developed and positively evaluated: *GrayArea*, in which users can manually demote unimportant information items to a gray area at the bottom of the folder; *DMTR*, which automatically demotes mobile phone contacts that have not been used for over six months; and *Old'nGray*, which automatically demotes old versions of documents so that users can spot the newest version at a glance.

Chapter 11 presented the *subjective project classification principle*, which states that all information items related to the same project should be stored together regardless of their technological format. This is implemented in the *single hierarchy* design scheme, in which there is only one folder hierarchy for all information items in a project, instead of the three existing hierarchies (for files, emails, and web favorites).

Chapter 12 introduced the *subjective context principle*, which states that information should be retrieved and viewed in the same context in which it was previously used. We have developed and positively evaluated five designs related to different context types: *ChittyChatty*, through which a user can straightforwardly retrieve his or her lecture notes (internal context) associated with a recorded lecture; *ItemHistory*, which allows a user to easily retrieve files, emails, and web pages that were previously open concurrently with a given information item (external context); *ContactMap*, which organizes personal information according to its social context, and *PiccyChatty*, which uses social information to infer the relative importance of different information items (both exploit social context); and *Starlight*, which automatically notifies a user when the deadline for an important actionable message approaches (temporal context).

We conclude with some thoughts regarding future research and technology for curation. Curation will continue to be a significant problem and will even be exacerbated. The size of people's personal archives continues to grow as new types of personal data and systems play even greater roles in our everyday lives. As a result, we believe that users will confront even greater challenges of organizing their personal information. Let's first talk about emerging technology and then discuss PIM theory and methods.

Technical Developments and Challenges

A recurrent theme of this book has been the failure of efforts to directly import technology from other domains to PIM. Part II documented how search, tagging, and GIM approaches have been repeatedly unsuccessful when applied to curation. These failures of imported techniques prompted us to propose the user-subjective approach covered in part III.

Although other technical approaches may yet bear fruit, this book has shown that many of the most successful PIM designs employ user-subjective design principles. Part III also suggested future PIM system designs that follow user-subjective guidelines. Some have already been evaluated, whereas we hope to develop and evaluate others (such as DupliPix, ItemHistory, and ProjectFolders) in the near future. More importantly, we hope that the user-subjective approach can provide a general future focus for design-oriented research in PIM. We hope that the demonstrated prior success of the user-subjective approach will lead other designers to exploit our principles in order to design their own novel PIM technologies. There are many promising directions here, including the use of AI techniques (as instantiated in StarLight), exploiting sensors (as in PiccyChatty), and using social information (as in ContactMap and PiccyChatty). Other designs may use simple direct manipulation approaches (as in GrayArea).

However, an additional future challenge for the user-subjective approach is to move beyond successful demonstrations of new PIM designs to having such designs deployed and incorporated in real-life systems that benefit real users outside our labs. We hope that commercial PIM systems manufacturers will read this book and be inspired to pick up the baton. We believe that user-subjective principles will continue to generate successful PIM systems designs and hope that they will be widely deployed.

Now, let's discuss other promising future technologies. When evaluating the usefulness of these technologies, we need to reemphasize prior experiences of failure. We are strong advocates of exploring new technologies to address PIM problems, but it is critical to evaluate their utility against existing technologies, given that the history of PIM is littered with examples of intuitively promising technologies that have not succeeded.

Machine Learning and the Semantic Desktop

It is apparent that people have massive amounts of personal information but limited time and inclination to organize it. Part I documented how people build up huge photo collections that are extremely poorly organized, for example, with negative consequences for retrieval. One obvious solution is to use machine-learning methods to organize all our personal data automatically, a concept known as the *semantic desktop*. Although this idea has been proposed many times and various technologies developed, we do not know of an actual, successful deployment with a real user population.

However, a less ambitious variant of this approach is to conduct automatic analysis of personal archives, allowing files to be tagged with metadata that may facilitate retrieval. For example, photos might be analyzed for location information, or facial recognition might be used to label photos with the names of specific people. Although these approaches are being explored in cloud deployments, such as Facebook/iPhoto photo tagging, we think there are challenges in the PIM context. One clear disadvantage of automatic approaches for PIM is that they remove the need for active user organization, which we have seen plays an important part in facilitating successful retrieval. However, such metadata might be usefully integrated into existing hierarchical organization—for example, to allow sorting of photos by person or place within a folder.

Predictive Algorithms

In part I, we reported a bias toward retrieval of highly recent information (Cutrell et al. 2006; Dumais et al. 2003; Fitchett, Cockburn, and Gutwin 2013). This is exploited by features such as History and the Back button for web retrieval, and the Recent Documents list, which helps to reduce file retrieval time (Fitchett and Cockburn 2015). This direction has been further explored by Cockburn and his colleagues. They first developed a successful algorithm that predicted users' next actions, including file accesses (Fitchett and Cockburn 2012). They then combined this with navigation and search (Fitchett, Cockburn, and Gutwin 2013), finding that this combined method reduced retrieval time in a longitudinal field study (Fitchett, Cockburn, and Gutwin 2014). We expect this approach will lead to further improvements in retrieval—for example, by adding a contextualized recent document list to navigation windows (in which the list predicts files within a folder and its subfolders) so that all major retrieval methods (navigation, search, and recent documents) are available in the same window.

Actionable Technology

Most PIM research has addressed informative items, targeting cases in which information is accessed intentionally by users when they need it. Less attention has been paid to reminding and techniques for retrieving actionable items that have specific deadlines, and few attempts to build task-management software have been successful (Bellotti et al. 2003; Dragunov et al. 2005). Notable exceptions are the boomerang add-in for Gmail (http://www.boomeranggmail.com/), and more recently Inbox by Gmail. Both allow users to "snooze" their actionable emails, so they remain invisible until their deadline approaches and thus avoid inbox clutter. A related promising direction is adding automated assistants to calendars (Bank et al. 2012). These allow users to define goals and automatically schedule time for them by spotting free slots in their schedules. This technique was recently released publicly in Google Calendar Goals.

Group Information Management Technologies

GIM is seeing massive growth with the emergence of new technologies such as Dropbox, Google Drive, and OneDrive. The prevalence of collaboration and the ready accessibility of computer networks mean that shared repositories are becoming ever more common. Part II documented problems that people experience with GIM technologies in creating shared organizations that are mutually accessible; new technologies are needed. Here and elsewhere, we have proposed that these technologies may involve social structuring following the user-subjective context principle (Kalnikaité and Whittaker 2008b). Other technical approaches might involve hybrids of PIM and GIM that allow personal views into publicly shared data, combining the benefits of shared storage with active personal organization and retrieval.

MultiDevice Capture and Retrieval

We are increasingly using multiple devices to generate and retrieve personal information. One important implication is that personal information is increasingly distributed across many different devices, making retrieval more complex. We saw in our studies of photo retrieval in chapter 4 that users already have problems in determining on which device a specific photo was located. Locating the correct device for retrieval is exacerbated if we add tablets and phones to possible devices, along with possible future technologies such as digital watches or wearable technologies like Google Glass. Networking these devices together could improve the situation, but it is a considerable technical challenge to unify all of a user's devices and applications. A second implication of device proliferation is that some curation behaviors will likely be device dependent. For example, both management and retrieval behaviors on a mobile phone are affected by limited display size, ease of text input, and other interactional resources (Bao et al. 2011).

Lifelogging and Quantified Self

Another important trend is the emergence of massive archives of automatically logged personal data generated by wearable devices, such as smartphones, cameras, and watches, along with fitness and other health-related applications. Such data includes heart rate, skin conductivity, steps, location, and automatically captured image data. Together, this data is sometimes termed the *quantified self*, or *lifelogging*. Although this data is clearly personal, it is passively captured and often low level, making it different from the types of personal data described in this book. Advocates of lifelogging make general arguments that such data will allow us to "remember everything" (Bell and Gemmell 2009), claims that we have critiqued elsewhere (Kalnikaité et al. 2010). There are also important unresolved questions about what we do with all this data and what value and insights it can bring us (Sellen and Whittaker 2010).

Nevertheless, there are exciting opportunities that this technology offers that might directly address issues discussed in this book. For example, wearables might allow users to easily generate user-subjective context (e.g., rich records associated with activities conducted at the time files were created), offering compelling new designs that address an important retrieval problem.

PIM Best Practices

People are constantly looking for ways to impove their PIM technologies and strategies, and we (the authors) are frequently asked to provide advice. However, we believe that research should be very careful in recommending "good practice." First it is difficult to measure whether a practice is good or not. More importantly, as we have seen in chapter 3, individual differences are prevalent in PIM, so that even if a practice is good for some people, research still needs to provide evidence that it will be good for others who implement the same practice. For this reason, we refrain from giving practical advice in this book. This is not to say that users cannot use the experience of others to elaborate and improve their own PIM strategies. Jones et al. (2015) describe a Delphi method study in which PIM researchers identified thirty-six key PIM practices and provided pros and cons for using each. We believe that allowing users to broaden their horizons with novel technologies and alternative strategies is a positive direction. Users can then decide which practices to adopt and which to ignore. This educational scheme can be combined with formal evaluations to determine which practices are adopted, as well as reasons for their success or lack of adoption.

Promising Research Directions

Expanding Our Methods

Our review in part I showed that PIM research so far has often been exploratory and phenomenon oriented when studying user behaviors, with early work relying on interviews and observational studies. Such methods were important for qualitative understanding of basic PIM phenomena but now need to be supported by more quantitative approaches (Kelly and Teevan 2007).

However, designing informative controlled tasks is problematic in PIM. PIM is fundamentally concerned with the retrieval of *personal* data, which means that there is limited utility for artificial, lab-based tasks in which people are asked to store and retrieve artificial items or carry out tasks imposed by the experimenter. This led us to propose the seminaturalistic EPIR procedure, in which participants are asked to retrieve personal items from their own systems (Bergman et al. 2010; Bergman, Whittaker, and Falk 2014; Whittaker, Bergman, and Clough 2010; Bergman, Tene-Rubinstein, and Shalom 2013; Bergman et al. 2013a). The EPIR approach addresses retrieval, but it might be extended to study different phases of the curation life cycle. One promising approach to studying management has been the use of automatic methods to analyze structure (Massey et al. 2014; Henderson and Srinivasan 2009; Gonçalves and Jorge 2003). We also believe that logfile approaches can be highly informative (Fitchett and Cockburn 2015; Dumais et al. 2003; Whittaker et al. 2011), although we are aware that sensitivity has to be shown in deploying monitoring software on personal machines.

In addition to studying curation behaviors, we also need new methods for evaluating new designs and systems. Our approach to evaluating the user-subjective design principles involves implementation and evaluation of different prototypes that embody those principles, a costly process. Designing PIM systems that can be used in practical contexts is highly demanding. PIM systems are fundamental to everyday online activity; as a result, it is hard to design convincing operational experimental systems, because such systems must work well and be fully featured if users are to trust them enough to use for the duration of an experimental trial (Whittaker 2005; Bellotti et al. 2005).

New Conceptual Frameworks That Explain PIM Behaviors

Prior work on curation has taken an empirical rather than a theoretical approach. Many PIM studies *describe* existing curation behaviors, rather than trying to *explain* those behaviors. Furthermore, the set of behaviors studied has been limited, with a focus on management rather than keeping or exploitation and almost no exploration of the relations between these different curation processes.

Elsewhere, we have argued that there is a need for more studies addressing the relations among different aspects of the curation life cycle (Bergman 2013; Bergman et al. 2010; Whittaker et al. 2011). Management is a clear case in point: Rather than simply documenting different types of management strategies, we need to determine the implications of those strategies—in particular, their effects on retrieval—allowing us to show, for example, that shallow, broad file hierarchies improve retrieval efficiency and success (Bergman et al. 2010).

To assist with this, Bergman (2013) maps a space of fifteen key variables that characterize and account for the variety of PIM behaviors. Identifying and mapping these variables facilitates quantitative research and allows researchers to explore relations among different curation processes. For example, Bergman et al. (2010) demonstrated that folder depth and folder size were important in determining retrieval success and efficiency. Future research might extend this, for example, to explore whether these relationships are affected by archive age, archive size, and so forth. We believe that PIM research is currently moving from an initial stage of exploratory studies to more rigorous quantitative ones, and future studies that explore the relations between these variables will shed light on hidden PIM behaviors.

We believe that another very important contribution of this book has been to explain PIM phenomena in terms of psychology. We have documented various regularities in curation processes that can be explained by cognitive psychology. For example, the phenomenon of overkeeping can be understood in terms of prospect theory (Kahneman and Tversky 1979). We used that theory to explain that users are focused on information loss, overestimating the risks of deletion, and underestimating retrieval costs when making keeping decisions. We offered a different type of cognitive explanation for preferences for navigation over search in terms of information-processing demands. Search requires access to verbal working memory, whereas navigation relies on more primitive, locational brain processes. A repeated theme in part II was the critical importance of active organization when foldering, and cognitive psychology documents the importance of such active organization for future recall. In the same way, we argued that one challenge of GIM was the absence of such active personal organization and the problems of accessing structures created by others. Future PIM research could explore further synergies with cognitive science.

In Closing

We believe that these are critical challenges to address. Curation is at the heart of everyday computer use, and is fundamental to much of what we do online. We hope that this book provides the scientific basis and inspiration for others to contribute transformational methods, technologies, and theories to this exciting area.

Notes

1 Personal Archives and Curation Processes

1. *Direct manipulation* is an approach to designing interactive computer interfaces that involves continuous representation of objects of interest and rapid, reversible, and incremental actions and feedback (Shneiderman 1982).

6 The Tagging Alternative

1. Retrieved from the Official Gmail Blog at http://gmailblog.blogspot .com/2010/04/new-in-labs-nested-labels-and-message.html on January 5, 2016.

11 The Subjective Project Classification Principle

1. We chose to use the term *projects* because it is general, because projects are typically of a longitudinal nature, and because this is the term used in the PIM literature. However, it is largely synonymous with other terms, such as *activities*, *tasks*, and *events* (Balakrishnan, Matthews, and Moran 2010; Yarosh et al. 2009; Dragunov et al. 2005).

2. This reminds us of an old science fiction story we read (but sadly couldn't locate), in which a galaxy was suffering religious wars. There were a thousand religions in the galaxy, each claiming to be the true

one, so they were in constant conflict. In this story, each of the thousand religions sent a wise man to a distant planet. For a year, these wise men argued, until they reached an agreement on a religion that was truly enlightened, because it contained elements from each of the thousand religions that preceded it. That moment was very important in the history of the galaxy—because from that moment on, there were no longer one thousand religions in the galaxy. There were 1,001.

12   The Subjective Context Principle

1. Project and importance are also context related, but they are presented separately for the sake of convenience.

References

Abrams, David, Ron Baecker, and Mark Chignell. 1998. "Information Archiving with Bookmarks: Personal Web Space Construction and Organization." In *Proceedings of the SIGCHI Conference on Human Factors in Computing Systems*, 41–48. New York: ACM Press/Addison-Wesley Publishing Co.

Adar, Eytan, David R. Karger, and Lynn Andrea Stein. 1999. "Haystack: Per-User Information Environments." In *Proceedings of the 8th International Conference on Information and Knowledge Management*, 413–422. New York: ACM Press.

Adrian, B., L. Sauermann, and T. Roth-Berghofer. 2007. "ConTag: A Semantic Tag Recommendation System." In *Proceedings of I-Semantics '07: The 3rd International Conference on Semantic Technologies*, ed. T. Pellegrini and S. Schaffert, 297–304. New York: ACM Press.

Agrawal, Rakesh, Roberto J. Bayardo, and Ramakrishnan Srikant. 2000. "Athena: Mining-Based Interactive Management of Text Database." In *Proceedings of the 7th International Conference on Extending Database Technology: Advances in Database Technology*, 365–379. Berlin: Springer-Verlag.

Aguirre, Geoffrey K., John A. Detre, David C. Alsop, and Mark D'Esposito. 1996. "The Parahippocampus Subserves Topographical Learning in Man." *Cerebral Cortex* 6 (6): 823–829.

Ajzen, Icek. 2002. "Perceived Behavioral Control, Self-Efficacy, Locus of Control, and the Theory of Planned Behavior." *Journal of Applied Social Psychology* 32 (4): 665–683.

Anderson, Janna Quitney, and Harrison Rainie. 2012. *The Future of Cloud Computing.* Washington, DC: Pew Internet and American Life Project.

Aula, Anne, Natalie Jhaveri, and Mika Kaki. 2005. "Information Search and Re-access Strategies of Experienced Web Users." In *Proceedings of the 14th International Conference on World Wide Web*, 583–592. New York: ACM Press.

Baddeley, A. D. 1992. "Working Memory." *Science* 255 (5044): 556–559. doi:10.1126/science.1736359.

Baddeley, A. D. 1997. *Human Memory: Theory and Practice.* Hove, UK: Psychology Press.

Balakrishnan, Aruna D., Tara Matthews, and Thomas P. Moran. 2010. "Fitting an Activity-Centric System into an Ecology of Workplace Tools." In *Proceedings of the SIGCHI Conference on Human Factors in Computing Systems*, 787–790. New York: ACM Press.

Bälter, Olle. 2000. "Keystroke Level Analysis of Email Message Organization." In *Proceedings of the SIGCHI Conference on Human Factors in Computing Systems*, 105–112. New York: ACM Press.

Bank, Jacob, Zachary Cain, Yoav Shoham, Caroline Suen, and Dan Ariely. 2012. "Turning Personal Calendars into Scheduling Assistants." In *Proceedings of CHI '12 Extended Abstracts on Human Factors in Computing Systems*, 2667–2672. New York: ACM Press.

Bao, Patti, Jeffrey Pierce, Stephen Whittaker, and Shumin Zhai. 2011. "Smart Phone Use by Non-mobile Business Users." In *Proceedings of the 13th International Conference on Human Computer Interaction with Mobile Devices and Services*, 445–454. New York: ACM Press.

Barreau, Deborah K. 1995. "Context as a Factor in Personal Information Management Systems." *Journal of the American Society for Information Science* 46 (5): 327–339.

Barreau, Deborah K., and Bonnie A. Nardi. 1995. "Finding and Reminding: File Organization from the Desktop." *SIGCHI Bulletin* 27 (3): 39–43.

Bek, Judith, Mark Blades, Michael Siegal, and Rosemary Varley. 2010. "Language and Spatial Reorientation: Evidence from Severe Aphasia." *Journal of Experimental Psychology: Learning, Memory, and Cognition* 36 (3): 646–658.

Belkin, Nicholas J. 1980. "Anomalous States of Knowledge as a Basis for Information Retrieval." *Canadian Journal of Information Science—Revue canadienne des sciences de l'information* 5 (May): 133–143.

Bell, C. Gordon, and Jim Gemmell. 2009. *Total Recall: How the E-Memory Revolution Will Change Everything.* New York: Dutton.

Bellotti, Victoria, Nicolas Ducheneaut, Mark Howard, and Ian Smith. 2003. "Taking Email to Task: The Design and Evaluation of a Task Management Centered Email Tool." In *Proceedings of the SIGCHI Conference on Human Factors in Computing Systems*, 345–352. New York: ACM Press.

Bellotti, Victoria, Nicolas Ducheneaut, Mark Howard, Ian Smith, and Rebecca E. Grinter. 2005. "Quality versus Quantity: E-Mail-Centric Task Management and Its Relation with Overload." *Human–Computer Interaction* 20:89–138.

Bellotti, Victoria, and Ian Smith. 2000. "Informing the Design of an Information Management System with Iterative Fieldwork." In *Proceedings of the Conference on Designing Interactive Systems: Processes, Practices, Methods, and Techniques*, 227–237. New York: ACM Press.

Benn, Yael, Ofer Bergman, Liv Glazer, Paris Arent, Iain D. Wilkinson, Rosemary Varley, and Steve Whittaker. 2015. "Navigating through Digital Folders Uses the Same Brain Structures as Real World Navigation." *Scientific Reports* 5:1–8.

Bentley, Frank, Crysta Metcalf, and Gunnar Harboe. 2006. "Personal vs. Commercial Content: The Similarities between Consumer Use of Photos and Music." In *Proceedings of the SIGCHI Conference on Human Factors in Computing Systems*, 667–676. New York: ACM Press.

Bergman, Ofer. 2006. "The Use of Subjective Attributes in Personal Information Management Systems." Ph.D. diss. (in Hebrew), School of Education, Tel Aviv University, Tel Aviv, Israel.

Bergman, Ofer. 2013. "Variables for Personal Information Management Research." *Aslib Proceedings* 65 (5): 464–483.

Bergman, Ofer, Ruth Beyth-Marom, Ahuva Leopold, Doron Hadar, and Amnon Dekel. 2000. "From 'Learning-by-Viewing' to 'Learning-by-Doing': A Video Annotation Educational Technology Tool." In *ED-MEDIA 2000*, 1555–1556. Charlottesville, AACE.

Bergman, Ofer, Ruth Beyth-Marom, and Rafi Nachmias. 2003. "The User-Subjective Approach to Personal Information Management Systems." *Journal of the American Society for Information Science and Technology* 54 (9): 872–878.

Bergman, Ofer, Ruth Beyth-Marom, and Rafi Nachmias. 2006. "The Project Fragmentation Problem in Personal Information Management." In *CHI 2006 Conference on Human Factors in Computing Systems*, 271–274. New York: ACM Press.

Bergman, Ofer, Ruth Beyth-Marom, and Rafi Nachmias. 2008. "The User-Subjective Approach to Personal Information Management Systems Design: Evidence and Implementations." *Journal of the American Society for Information Science and Technology* 59 (2): 235–246.

Bergman, Ofer, Ruth Beyth-Marom, Rafi Nachmias, Noa Gradovitch, and Steve Whittaker. 2008. "Improved Search Engines and Navigation Preference in Personal Information Management." *ACM Transactions on Information Systems* 26 (4): 1–24. doi:10.1145/1402256.1402259.

Bergman, Ofer, Oded Elyada, Noga Dvir, Yana Vaitzman, and Adir Ben Ami. 2015. "Spotting the Latest Version of a File with Old'nGray." *Interacting with Computers* 27 (6): 630–639. doi:10.1093/iwc/iwu018.

Bergman, Ofer, Noa Gradovitch, Judit Bar-Ilan, and Ruth Beyth-Marom. 2013a. "Folder vs. Tag Preference in Personal Information Management." *Journal of the American Society for Information Science and Technology* 64 (10): 1995–2012.

Bergman, Ofer, Noa Gradovitch, Judit Bar-Ilan, and Ruth Beyth-Marom. 2013b. "Tagging Personal Information: A Contrast between Attitudes and Behavior." In *Proceedings of the American Society for Information Science and Technology*, 1–8. New York: John Wiley & Sons.

Bergman, Ofer, Andreas Komninos, Dimitrios Liarokapis, and James Clarke. 2012. "You Never Call: Demoting Unused Contacts on Mobile Phones Using DMTR." *Personal and Ubiquitous Computing* 16 (6): 757–766. doi:10.1007/s00779-011-0411-3.

Bergman, Ofer, Maskit Tene-Rubinstein, and Jonathan Shalom. 2013. "The Use of Attention Resources in Navigation vs. Search." *Personal and Ubiquitous Computing* 17 (3): 583–590.

Bergman, Ofer, Simon Tucker, Ruth Beyth-Marom, Edward Cutrell, and Steve Whittaker. 2009. "It's Not That Important: Demoting Personal Information of Low Subjective Importance Using GrayArea." In *Proceedings of the Conference on Human Factors and Computing Systems*, 269–278. New York: ACM Press.

Bergman, Ofer, Steve Whittaker, and Noa Falk. 2014. "Shared Files: The Retrieval Perspective." *Journal of the American Society for Information Science and Technology* 65 (10): 1949–1963. doi:10.1002/asi.23147.

Bergman, Ofer, Steve Whittaker, Mark Sanderson, Rafi Nachmias, and Anand Ramamoorthy. 2010. "The Effect of Folder Structure on Personal File Navigation." *Journal of the American Society for Information Science and Technology* 61 (12): 2426–2441.

Bergman, Ofer, Steve Whittaker, Mark Sanderson, Rafi Nachmias, and Anand Ramamoorthy. 2012. "How Do We Find Personal Files? The Effect of OS, Presentation and Depth on File Navigation." In *Proceedings of the SIGCHI Conference on Human Factors in Computing Systems*, 2977–2980. New York: ACM Press.

Berlin, Lucy M., Robin Jeffries, Vicki L. O'Day, Andreas Paepcke, and Cathleen Wharton. 1993. "Where Did You Put It? Issues in the Design and Use of a Group Memory." In *Proceedings of the INTERACT '93 and CHI '93 Conference on Human Factors in Computing Systems*, 23–30. New York: ACM Press.

Bingman, Verner P., and Joy A. Mench. 1990. "Homing Behavior of Hippocampus and Parahippocampus Lesioned Pigeons Following Short-Distance Releases." *Behavioural Brain Research* 40 (3): 227–238.

Blanc-Brude, Tristan, and Dominique L. Scapin. 2007. "What Do People Recall about Their documents? Implications for Desktop Search Tools." In *Proceedings of the 12th International Conference on Intelligent User Interfaces*, 102–111. New York: ACM Press.

Blau, Maya, Shany Madmon, and Ofer Bergman. 2013. "The Effect of Computer Literacy on the Percentage of Personal File Search." In *Proceedings of the Chais Conference on Instructional Technologies Research 2013: Learning in the Technological Era*, 92–93. Raanana: The Open University of Israel.

Bloehdorn, Stephan, and Max Völkel. 2006. "Tagfs: Tag Semantics for Hierarchical File Systems." In *6th International Conference on Knowledge Management (I-KNOW 06)*, 1–6. New York: ACM Press.

Blunschi, Lukas, Jens-Peter Dittrich, Olivier René Girard, Shant Kirakos Karakashian, and Antonio Vaz Salles Marcos. 2007. "A Dataspace Odyssey: The iMeMex Personal Dataspace Management System." In *Conference on Innovative Data Systems Research*, 114–119. New York: ACM Press.

Boardman, Richard. 2004. "Improving Tool Support for Personal Information Management." Ph.D. diss., Imperial College, London.

Boardman, Richard, and M. Angela Sasse. 2004. "'Stuff Goes into the Computer and Doesn't Come Out': A Cross-Tool Study of Personal Information Management." Paper presented at the SIGCHI Conference on Human Factors in Computing Systems, Vienna, Austria, June 22–27.

Boardman, Richard, Robert Spence, and M. Angela Sasse. 2003. "Too Many Hierarchies? The Daily Struggle for Control of the Workspace." In *HCI International, Crete, Greece, 2003*, edited by Julie Jacko and Constantine Stephanidis, 616–620. Mahwah, NJ: Lawrence Erlbaum Associates.

Brewer, William F. 1988. "Memory for Randomly Sampled Autobiographical Events." In *Remembering Reconsidered: Ecological and Traditional*

Approaches to the Study of Memory, edited by Ulric Neisser and Eugene Winograd, 21–90. New York: Cambridge University Press.

Brown, John. 1958. "Some Tests of the Decay Theory of Immediate Memory." *Quarterly Journal of Experimental Psychology* 10:12–21.

Bruce, Harry. 2005. "Personal Anticipated Information Need." *Information Research* 10 (3). see http://www.informationr.net/ir/10-3/paper232 .html.

Bruce, Harry, William Jones, and Susan Dumais. 2004. "Information Behaviour That Keeps Found Things Found." *Information Research* 10 (1). http://www.informationr.net/ir/10-1/paper207.html.

Bush, Vannevar. 1945. "As We May Think." *Atlantic Monthly* 176 (1): 101–108.

Capra, Robert G., and Manuel A. Pérez-Quiñones. 2005. "Using Web Search Engines to Find and Refind Information." *Computer* 38 (10): 36–42.

Catledge, Lara D., and James E. Pitkow. 1995. "Characterizing Browsing Strategies in the World-Wide Web." *Computer Networks and ISDN Systems* 27 (6): 1065–1073.

Civan, Andrea, William Jones, Predrag Klasnja, and Harry Bruce. 2008. "Better to Organize Personal Information by Folders or by Tags? The Devil Is in the Details." In *Proceedings of the American Society for Information Science and Technology*, 1–13. Hoboken, NJ: John Wiley & Sons.

Cockburn, Andy, and Saul Greenberg. 2000. "Issues of Page Representation and Organisation in Web Browser's Revisitation Tools." *Australasian Journal of Information Systems* 7 (2): 120–127.

Collins, Allan M., and Elizabeth F. Loftus. 1975. "A Spreading-Activation Theory of Semantic Processing." *Psychological Review* 82 (6): 407–428.

Cornwell, Brian R., Linda L. Johnson, Tom Holroyd, Frederick W. Carver, and Christian Grillon. 2008. "Human Hippocampal and Para-hippocampal Theta during Goal-Directed Spatial Navigation Predicts

Performance on a Virtual Morris Water Maze." *Journal of Neuroscience* 28 (23): 5983–5990.

Craik, Fergus I. M., and Robert S. Lockhart. 1972. "Levels of Processing: A Framework for Memory Research." *Journal of Verbal Learning and Verbal Behavior* 11 (6): 671–684.

Cutrell, Edward, Susan T. Dumais, and Jaime Teevan. 2006. "Searching to Eliminate Personal Information Management." *Communications of the ACM* 49 (1): 58–64.

Cutrell, Edward, Daniel C. Robbins, Susan T. Dumais, and Raman Sarin. 2006. "Fast, Flexible Filtering with Phlat: Personal Search and Organization Made Easy." In *CHI 2006 Conference on Human Factors in Computing Systems*, 261–270. New York: ACM Press.

Czerwinski, Mary, Eric Horvitz, and Susan Wilhite. 2004. "A Diary Study of Task Switching and Interruptions." In *Proceedings of the SIGCHI Conference on Human Factors in Computing Systems*, 175–182. New York: ACM Press.

Dabbish, Laura A., Robert E. Kraut, Susan Fussell, and Sara Kiesler. 2005. "Understanding Email Use: Predicting Action on a Message." In *Proceedings of the SIGCHI Conference on Human Factors in Computing Systems*. New York: ACM Press.

Dekel, Amnon, and Ofer Bergman. 2000. "Synopsus: A Personal Summary Tool for Video." In *CHI '00 Extended Abstracts on Human Factors in Computing Systems*, 4–5. New York: ACM Press.

Dourish, Paul, W. Keith Edwards, Anthony LaMarca, John Lamping, Karin Petersen, Michael Salisbury, Douglas B. Terry, and James Thornton. 2000. "Extending Document Management Systems with User-Specific Active Properties." *ACM Transactions on Information Systems* 18 (2): 140–170.

Dourish, Paul, W. Keith Edwards, Anthony LaMarca, and Michael Salisbury. 1999. "Presto: An Experimental Architecture for Fluid Interactive Document Spaces." *ACM Transactions on Computer–Human Interaction* 6 (2): 133–161.

Dragunov, Anton N., Thomas G. Dietterich, Kevin Johnsrude, Matthew McLaughlin, Lida Li, and Jonathan L. Herlocker. 2005. "TaskTracer: A Desktop Environment to Support Multi-Tasking Knowledge Workers." In *Proceedings of the 10th International Conference on Intelligent User Interfaces*, 75–82. New York: ACM Press.

du Boisgueheneuc, Foucaud, Richard Levy, Emmanuelle Volle, Magali Seassau, Hughes Duffau, Serge Kinkingnehun, Yves Samson, Sandy Zhang, and Bruno Dubois. 2006. "Functions of the Left Superior Frontal Gyrus in Humans: A Lesion Study." *Brain* 129 (12): 3315–3328.

Ducheneaut, Nicolas, and Victoria Bellotti. 2001. "E-Mail as Habitat: An Exploration of Embedded Personal Information Management." *interactions* 8 (5): 30–38.

Dumais, Susan T., Edward Cutrell, J. J. Cadiz, Gavin Jancke, Raman Sarin, and Daniel C. Robbins. 2003. "Stuff I've Seen: A System for Personal Information Retrieval and Re-Use." In *Proceedings of the 26th Annual International ACM SIGIR Conference on Research and Development in Information Retrieval*, 72–79. New York: ACM Press.

Dumais, Susan T., and Thomas K. Landauer. 1983. "Using Examples to Describe Categories." In *Proceedings of the SIGCHI Conference on Human Factors in Computing Systems*, 112–115. New York: ACM Press.

Ellis, David, and Merete Haugan. 1997. "Modelling the Information Seeking Patterns of Engineers and Research Scientists in an Industrial Environment." *Journal of Documentation* 53 (4): 384–403.

Elsweiler, David. 2008. "Supporting Human Memory in Personal Information Management." *SIGIR Forum* 42 (1): 75–76. doi: 10.1145/1394251.1394270.

Elsweiler, David, Mark Baillie, and Ian Ruthven. 2008. "Exploring Memory in Email Refinding." *ACM Transactions on Information Systems* 26 (4): 1–36. doi:10.1145/1402256.1402260.

Elsweiler, David, Mark Baillie, and Ian Ruthven. 2011. "What Makes Re-finding Information Difficult? A Study of Email Re-finding." In *Advances in Information Retrieval*, 568–579. Berlin: Springer.

Epstein, Russell, and Nancy Kanwisher. 1998. "A Cortical Representation of the Local Visual Environment." *Nature* 392 (6676): 598–601.

Erickson, Thomas. 2006. "From PIM to GIM: Personal Information Management in Group Contexts." *Communications of the ACM* 49 (1): 74–75. doi: 10.1145/1107458.1107495.

Farina, Paula A. 2005. "A Comparison of Two Desktop Search Engines: Google Desktop Search (Beta) vs. Windows XP Search Companion." In *21st Computer Science Seminar*. Hartford.

Fertig, Scott, Eric Freeman, and David Gelernter. 1996a. "'Finding and Reminding' Reconsidered." *SIGCHI Bulletin* 28 (1): 66–69.

Fertig, Scott, Eric Freeman, and David Gelernter. 1996b. "Lifestreams: An Alternative to the Desktop Metaphor." In *Conference Companion on Human Factors in Computing Systems: Common Ground*, 410–411. New York: ACM Press.

Fisher, Danyel, A. J. Brush, Eric Gleave, and Marc A. Smith. 2006. "Revisiting Whittaker and Sidner's 'Email Overload' Ten Years Later." In *Proceedings of the 2006 20th Anniversary Conference on Computer Supported Cooperative Work*. New York: ACM Press.

Fitchett, Stephen, and Andy Cockburn. 2012. "Accessrank: Predicting What Users Will Do Next." In *Proceedings of the SIGCHI Conference on Human Factors in Computing Systems*, 2239–2242. New York: ACM Press.

Fitchett, Stephen, and Andy Cockburn. 2015. "An Empirical Characterisation of File Retrieval." *International Journal of Human–Computer Studies* 74:1–13.

Fitchett, Stephen, Andy Cockburn, and Carl Gutwin. 2013. "Improving Navigation-Based File Retrieval." In *Proceedings of the SIGCHI Conference on Human Factors in Computing Systems Systems*, 2329–2338. New York: ACM Press.

Fitchett, Stephen, Andy Cockburn, and Carl Gutwin. 2014. "Finder Highlights: Field Evaluation and Design of an Augmented File Browser." In *Proceedings of the 32nd Annual ACM Conference on Human Factors in Computing Systems*, 3685–3694. New York: ACM Press.

Freeman, Eric, and David Gelernter. 1996. "Lifestreams: A Storage Model for Personal Data." *SIGMOD Record* 25 (1): 80–86. doi: 10.1145/381854.381893.

Frohlich, David, Allan Kuchinsky, Celine Pering, Abbe Don, and Steven Ariss. 2002. "Requirements for Photoware." In *Proceedings of the 2002 ACM Conference on Computer Supported Cooperative Work*, 166–175. New York: ACM Press.

Furnas, George W., Caterina Fake, Luis von Ahn, Joshua Schachter, Scott Golder, Kevin Fox, Marc Davis, Cameron Marlow, and Mor Naaman. 2006. "Why Do Tagging Systems Work?" In *CHI '06 Extended Abstracts on Human Factors in Computing Systems*. New York: ACM Press.

Furtak, Sharon C., Shau-Ming Wei, Kara L. Agster, and Rebecca D. Burwell. 2007. "Functional Neuroanatomy of the Parahippocampal Region in the Rat: The Perirhinal and Postrhinal Cortices." *Hippocampus* 17 (9): 709–722.

Furuya, Yoichi, Jumpei Matsumoto, Etsuro Hori, Cyrus Villas Boas, Anh Hai Tran, Yutaka Shimada, Taketoshi Ono, and Hisao Nishijo. 2014. "Place-Related Neuronal Activity in the Monkey Parahippocampal Gyrus and Hippocampal Formation during Virtual Navigation." *Hippocampus* 24 (1): 113–130.

Gao, Qin. 2011. "An Empirical Study of Tagging for Personal Information Organization: Performance, Workload, Memory, and Consistency." *International Journal of Human–Computer Interaction* 27 (9): 821–863. doi: 10.1080/10447318.2011.555309.

Gemmell, Jim, Gordon Bell, Roger Lueder, Steven Drucker, and Curtis Wong. 2002. "MyLifeBits: Fulfilling the Memex Vision." In *Proceedings of the 10th ACM International Conference on Multimedia*, 235–238. New York: ACM Press.

Gilbert, Daniel. 2009. *Stumbling on Happiness*. New York: Random House.

Golder, Scott A., and Bernardo A. Huberman. 2006. "Usage Patterns of Collaborative Tagging Systems." *Journal of Information Science* 32 (2): 198–208.

Gonçalves, Daniel, and Joaquim A. Jorge. 2003. "An Empirical Study of Personal Document Spaces." In *Proceedings of DSV-I S '03*, 46–60. Berlin: Springer.

Gonçalves, Daniel, and Joaquim A. Jorge. 2004. "Describing Documents: What Can Users Tell Us?" In *Proceedings of the 9th International Conference on Intelligent User Interfaces*, 247–249. New York ACM Press.

González, Victor M., and Gloria Mark. 2004. "Constant, Constant, Multi-Tasking Craziness: Managing Multiple Working Spheres." In *Proceedings of the SIGCHI Conference on Human Factors in Computing Systems*, 113–120. New York: ACM Press.

Granovetter, Mark S. 1973. "The Strength of Weak Ties." *American Journal of Sociology* 78 (6):1360–1380.

Groza, Tudor, Siegfried Handschuh, and Knud Moeller. 2007. "The NEPOMUK Project: On the Way to the Social Semantic Desktop." In *Proceedings of I-Semantics '07: The 3rd International Conference on Semantic Technologies*, ed. T. Pellegrini and S. Schaffert, 1–12. New York: ACM Press.

Gutwin, Carl, Mark Roseman, and Saul Greenberg. 1996. "A Usability Study of Awareness Widgets in a Shared Workspace Groupware System." In *Proceedings of the 1996 ACM Conference on Computer Supported Cooperative Work*, 258–267. New York: ACM Press.

Gwizdka, Jacek. 2004a. "Cognitive Abilities and Email Interaction: Impacts of Interface and Task." Ph.D. diss., University of Toronto, Canada.

Gwizdka, Jacek. 2004b. "Email Task Management Styles: The Cleaners and the Keepers." In *CHI '04 Extended Abstracts on Human Factors in Computing Systems*, 1235–1238. New York: ACM Press.

Gwizdka, Jacek. 2010. "Distribution of Cognitive Load in Web Search." *Journal of the American Society for Information Science and Technology* 61 (11): 2167–2187.

Gwizdka, Jacek, and Mark Chignell. 2007. "Individual Differences." In *Personal Information Management*, edited by William Jones and Jaime Teevan, 206–220. Seattle: University of Washington Press.

Heckner, Markus, Michael Heilemann, and Christian Wolff. 2009. "Personal Information Management vs. Resource Sharing: Towards a Model of Information Behaviour in Social Tagging Systems." In *Third International AAAI Conference on Weblogs and Social Media, ICWSM-09*, 42–49. San Jose, CA: AAAI.

Henderson, Sarah, and A. Srinivasan. 2009. "An Empirical Analysis of Personal Digital Document Structures." In *HCI International 2009*, 394–403. Berlin: Springer.

Hill, William C., and James D. Hollan. 1994. "History-Enriched Digital Objects: Prototypes and Policy Issues." *Information Society* 10 (2): 139–145.

Hill, William C., James D. Hollan, Dave Wroblewski, and Tim McCandless. 1992. "Edit Wear and Read Wear." In *Proceedings of the SIGCHI Conference on Human Factors in Computing Systems*, 3–9. New York: ACM Press.

Hinds, Pamela. 2002. *Distributed Work*. Cambridge, MA: MIT Press.

Hsieh, Ji Lung, Hsun Chen Chien, I. Wen Lin, and Chuen Tsai Sun. 2008. "A Web-Based Tagging Tool for Organizing Personal Documents on PCs." In *International Conference of Computer–Human Interaction 2008*, 1–6. New York: ACM Press.

Ingwersen, P. 1996. "Cognitive Perspectives of Information Retrieval Interaction: Elements of a Cognitive IR Theory." *Journal of Documentation* 52 (1): 3–50.

John, O. P. 1990. "The 'Big Five' Factor Taxonomy: Dimensions of Personality in the Natural Language and in Questionnaires." In *Handbook of Personality: Theory and Research*, edited by L. Pervin, 66–100. New York: Guilford Press.

Jones, William. 2004. "Finders, Keepers? The Present and Future Perfect in Support of Personal Information Management." *First Monday* 9 (3). http://firstmonday.org/ojs/index.php/fm/article/view/1123/1043.

Jones, William. 2007a. *Keeping Found Things Found: The Study and Practice of Personal Information Management*. Seattle: Morgan Kaufmann.

Jones, William. 2007b. "Personal Information Management." *Annual Review of Information Science and Technology* 41 (1): 453–504.

Jones, William. 2013. *The Future of Personal Information Management: Building Places of Our Own for Digital Information*. San Rafael, CA: Morgan and Claypool.

Jones, William, Harry Bruce, Marcia J. Bates, Nicholas Belkin, Ofer Bergman, and Cathy Marshall. 2005. "Personal Information Management in the Present and Future Perfect: Reports from a Special NSF-Sponsored Workshop." *Proceedings of the American Society for Information Science and Technology* 42 (1). doi: 10.1002/meet.1450420151.

Jones, W., R. Capra, A. Diekema, J. Teevan, M. Pérez-Quiñones, J. D. Dinneen, and B. Hemminger. 2015. "'For Telling' the Present: Using the Delphi Method to Understand Personal Information Management Practices." In *Proceedings of the 33rd Annual ACM Conference on Human Factors in Computing Systems*, 513–522. New York: ACM Press.

Jones, William, and Susan T. Dumais. 1986. "The Spatial Metaphor for User Interfaces: Experimental Tests of Reference by Location versus Name." *ACM Transactions on Information Systems* 4 (1): 42–63. doi:10.1145/5401.5405.

Jones, William, David Karger, Ofer Bergman, Mike Franklin, Wanda Pratt, and Marcia Bates. 2005. *Towards a Unification and Integration of PIM Support*. Seattle: National Science Foundation.

Jones, William, Charles F. Munat, and Harry Bruce. 2005. "The Universal Labeler: Plan the Project and Let Your Information Follow." In *Proceedings of the American Society for Information Science and Technology*, 1–12. Hoboken, NJ: John Wiley & Sons.

Jones, William, Ammy Jiranida Phuwanartnurak, Rajdeep Gill, and Harry Bruce. 2005. "Don't Take My Folders Away! Organizing Personal Information to Get Things Done." In *CHI '05 Extended Abstracts on Human Factors in Computing Systems*. New York: ACM Press.

Jones, William, and Jaime Teevan. 2007. *Personal Information Management*. Seattle: University of Washington Press.

Kahneman, Daniel, and Amos Tversky. 1979. *Prospect Theory: An Analysis of Decision Making under Risk*. New York: The Econometric Society.

Kalnikaité, Vaiva, Abigail Sellen, Steve Whittaker, and David Kirk. 2010. "Now Let Me See Where I Was: Understanding How Lifelogs Mediate Memory." In *Proceedings of the SIGCHI Conference on Human Factors in Computing Systems*, 2045–2054. New York: ACM Press.

Kalnikaité, Vaiva, and Steve Whittaker. 2007. "Software or Wetware? Discovering When and Why People Use Digital Prosthetic Memory." In *Proceedings of the SIGCHI Conference on Human Factors in Computing Systems*, 71–80. New York: ACM Press.

Kalnikaité, Vaiva, and Steve Whittaker. 2008a. "Cueing Digital Memory: How and Why Do Digital Notes Help Us Remember?" In *Proceedings of the 22nd British HCI Group Annual Conference on HCI 2008: People and Computers XXII: Culture, Creativity, Interaction*, volume 1, 153–161. Swinton, UK: British Computer.

Kalnikaité, Vaiva, and Steve Whittaker. 2008b. "Social Summarization: Does Social Feedback Improve Access to Speech Data?" In *Proceedings of the 2008 ACM Conference on Computer Supported Cooperative Work*, 9–12. New York: ACM Press.

Kalnikaité, Vaiva, and Steve Whittaker. 2010. "Beyond Being There? Evaluating Augmented Digital Records." *International Journal of Human–Computer Studies* 68 (10): 627–640.

Kaptelinin, Victor. 2003. "UMEA: Translating Interaction Histories into Project Contexts." In *Proceedings of the SIGCHI Conference on Human Factors in Computing Systems*, 353–360. New York: ACM Press.

Karger, David R., and Dennis Quan. 2004. "Collections: Flexible, Essential Tools for Information Management." In *CHI '04 Extended Abstracts on Human Factors in Computing Systems*, 1159–1162. New York: ACM Press.

Karlson, Amy K., Greg Smith, and Bongshin Lee. 2011. "Which Version Is This? Improving the Desktop Experience within a Copy-Aware Computing Ecosystem." In *Proceedings of the 2011 Annual Conference on Human Factors in Computing Systems*, 2669–2678. New York: ACM Press.

Kelly, Diane, and Jaime Teevan. 2007. "Understanding What Works: Evaluating PIM Tools." In *Personal Information Management*, edited by P. Jones William and Jaime Teevan, 190–204. Seattle: University of Washington Press.

Kidd, Alison. 1994. "The Marks Are on the Knowledge Worker." In *Proceedings of the SIGCHI Conference on Human Factors in Computing Systems: Celebrating Interdependence*, 186–191. New York: ACM Press.

Kim, Y. M., and S. Y. Rieh. 2005. "Dual-Task Performance as a Measure for Mental Effort in Library Searching and Web Searching." In *68th Annual Meeting of the American Society for Information Science and Technology (ASIST 2008)*, 1–25. Hoboken, NJ: John Wiley & Sons.

Kirk, David, Abigail Sellen, Carsten Rother, and Ken Wood. 2006. "Understanding Photowork." In *SIGCHI Conference on Human Factors in Computing Systems*, 761–770. New York: ACM Press.

Kobayashi, Mei, and Koichi Takeda. 2000. "Information Retrieval on the Web." ACM Computing Surveys 32 (2): 144–173. doi: 10.1145/358923.358934.

Kuhlthau, Carol C. 1991. "Inside the Search Process: Information Seeking from the User's Perspective." *JASIS* 42 (5): 361–371.

Kuny, T. 1997. "A Digital Dark Ages? Challenges in the Preservation of Electronic Information." Paper presented at the 63rd IFLA Council and General Conference, Copenhagen, Denmark, August 31–September 5.

Kwasnik, Barbara H. 1991. "The Importance of Factors That Are Not Document Attributes in the Organization of Personal Documents." *Journal of Documentation* 47:389–398.

Lansdale, Mark W. 1988. "The Psychology of Personal Information Management." *Applied Ergonomics* 19 (1): 55–66.

Lansdale, Mark W., and Ernest Edmonds. 1992. "Using Memory for Events in the Design of Personal Filing Systems." *International Journal of Man–Machine Studies* 36 (1): 97–126.

Lesk, Michael. 1998. "Preserving Digital Objects: Recurrent Needs and Challenges."

Linton, M. 1982. "Transformations of Memory in Everyday Life." In *Memory Observed: Remembering in Natural Context*, edited by Ulric Neisser, 77–91. San Francisco: Freeman.

Lowe, Michael. 2006. *Evaluation of Desktop Search Applications*. Sydney, Australia: Kalio.

Lutters, W. G., M. S. Ackerman, and X. Zhou. 2007. "Group Information Management." In *Personal Information Management*, edited by William Jones and Jaime Teevan, 236–248. Seattle: University of Washington Press.

Ma, Shanshan, and Susan Wiedenbeck. 2009. "File Management with Hierarchical Folders and Tags." In *Proceedings of the 27th International Conference Extended Abstracts on Human Factors in Computing Systems*, 3745–3750. New York: ACM Press.

Maes, P. 1994. "Agents That Reduce Work and Information Overload." *Communications of the ACM* 37 (7): 30–40.

Maguire, Eleanor, Richard S. J. Frackowiak, and Christopher D. Frith. 1996. "Learning to Find Your Way: A Role for the Human Hippocampal Formation." *Proceedings of the Royal Society of London: Series B: Biological Sciences* 263 (1377): 1745–1750.

Maguire, Eleanor, Richard S. J. Frackowiak, and Christopher D. Frith. 1997. "Recalling Routes around London: Activation of the Right Hippocampus in Taxi Drivers." *Journal of Neuroscience* 17 (18): 7103–7110.

Mahmud, Jalal, Tara Matthews, Steve Whittaker, Tom Moran, and Tessa Lau. 2011. "Topika: Integrating Collaborative Sharing with Email." In *Proceedings of the 2011 Annual Conference on Human Factors in Computing Systems*, 3161–3164. New York: ACM Press.

Malone, Thomas W. 1983. "How Do People Organize Their Desks? Implications for the Design of Office Information Systems." *ACM Transactions on Office Information Systems* 1:99–112.

Mandler, George. 1980. "Recognizing: The Judgment of Previous Occurrence." *Psychological Review* 87 (3): 252.

Marchionini, Gary. 1997. *Information Seeking in Electronic Environments.* Cambridge: Cambridge University Press.

Marsden, Gary, and David E. Cairns. 2003. "Improving the Usability of the Hierarchical File System." In *Proceedings of the 2003 Annual Research Conference of the South African Institute of Computer Scientists and Information Technologists on Enablement through Technology,* 122–129. New York: ACM Press.

Marshall, Catherine C. 2008a. "Rethinking Personal Digital Archiving, Part 1: Four Challenges from the Field." *D-Lib Magazine* 14 (3): 2.

Marshall, Catherine C. 2008b. "Rethinking Personal Digital Archiving, Part 2: Implications for Services, Applications, and Institutions." *D-Lib Magazine* 14 (3): 3.

Massey, Charlotte, Thomas Lennig, and Steve Whittaker. 2014. "Cloudy Forecast: An Exploration of the Factors Underlying Shared Repository Use." In *Proceedings of the 32nd Annual ACM Conference on Human Factors in Computing Systems,* 2461–2470. New York: ACM Press.

Massey, Charlotte, Sean TenBrook, Chaconne Tatum, and Steve Whittaker. 2014. "PIM and Personality: What Do Our Personal File Systems Say about Us?" In *Proceedings of the 32nd Annual ACM Conference on Human Factors in Computing Systems,* 3695–3704. New York: ACM Press.

Matthews, Tara, Steve Whittaker, Hernan Badenes, Barton A. Smith, Michael Muller, Kate Ehrlich, Michelle X. Zhou, and Tessa Lau. 2013. "Community Insights: Helping Community Leaders Enhance the Value of Enterprise Online Communities." In *Proceedings of the Conference on Human Factors in Computing Systems (CHI '13),* 513–522. New York: ACM Press.

Medlin, D. L., and M. M. Schaffer. 1978. "Context Theory of Classification Learning." *Psychological Review* 85:207–238.

Millen, David R., Jonathan Feinberg, and Bernard Kerr. 2006. "Dogear: Social Bookmarking in the Enterprise." In *Proceedings of the SIGCHI Conference on Human Factors in Computing Systems*, 111–120. New York: ACM Press.

Millen, David R., Meng Yang, Steven Whittaker, and Jonathan Feinberg. 2007. "Social Bookmarking and Exploratory Search." In *ECSCW 2007*, 21–40. Berlin: Springer.

Miller, G. 1956. "The Magical Number Seven, Plus or Minus Two: Some Limits on Our Capacity for Processing Information." *Psychological Review* 63 (2): 81–97.

Muller, Michael, David R. Millen, and Jonathan Feinberg. 2010. "Patterns of Usage in an Enterprise File-Sharing Service: Publicizing, Discovering, and Telling the News." In *Proceedings of the 28th International Conference on Human Factors in Computing Systems*, 763–766. New York: ACM Press.

Nardi, Bonnie A., Steve Whittaker, Ellen Isaacs, Mike Creech, Jeff Johnson, and John Hainsworth. 2002. "Integrating Communication and Information through ContactMap." *Communications of the ACM* 45 (4): 89–95.

Neisser, U. 1964. "Visual Search." *Scientific American* 210 (6): 94–102.

Neisser, U. 2014. *Cognitive Psychology: Classic Edition*. Oxford: Psychology Press.

Revisitation Revisited: Implications of a Long-Term Click-Stream Study of Browser Usage." In *Proceedings of the SIGCHI Conference on Human Factors in Computing Systems*, 597–606. New York: ACM Press.

Oleksik, Gerard, Max L. Wilson, Craig Tashman, Eduarda Mendes Rodrigues, Gabriella Kazai, Gavin Smyth, Natasa Milic-Frayling, and Rachel Jones. 2009. "Lightweight Tagging Expands Information and Activity Management Practices." In *27th International Conference on Human Factors in Computing Systems*, 279–288. New York: ACM Press.

Oliver, Nuria, Greg Smith, Chintan Thakkar, and Arun C. Surendran. 2006. "SWISH: Semantic Analysis of Window Titles and Switching History." In *Proceedings of the 11th International Conference on Intelligent User Interfaces*, 194–201. New York: ACM Press.

Pak, R., S. Pautz, and R. Iden. 2007. "Information Organization and Retrieval: An Assessment of Taxonomical and Tagging Systems." *Cognitive Technology* 12 (1): 31–44.

Park, Sang Cheol, and Sung Yul Ryoo. 2012. "An Empirical Investigation of End-Users Switching toward Cloud Computing: A Two Factor Theory Perspective." *Computers in Human Behavior* 29 (1): 160–170.

Peterson, L. R., and M. G. Peterson. 1959. "Short-Term Retention of Individual Verbal Items." *Journal of Experimental Psychology* 58 (3): 193–198.

Petrelli, Daniela, Steve Whittaker, and Jens Brockmeier. 2008. "AutoTopography: What Can Physical Mementos Tell Us about Digital Memories?" In *Proceedings of the SIGCHI Conference on Human Factors in Computing Systems*, 53–62. New York: ACM Press.

Pirolli, Peter. 2007. *Information Foraging Theory: Adaptive Interaction with Information*. New York: Oxford University Press.

Pirolli, Peter, and Stuart Card. 1995. "Information Foraging in Information Access Environments." In *Proceedings of the SIGCHI Conference on Human Factors in Computing Systems*, 51–58. New York: ACM Press/ Addison-Wesley Publishing Co.

Quan, Dennis, Karun Bakshi, David Huynh, and David R. Karger. 2003. "User Interfaces for Supporting Multiple Categorization." In *Proceedings of INTERACT 2003*, edited by M. Rauterberg, M. Menozzi, and J. Wesson, 228–235. Amsterdam: IOS Press.

Rader, Emilee. 2007. "Just Email It to Me! Why Things Get Lost in Shared File Repositories." Paper presented at GROUP'07 Doctoral Consortium, Sanibel Island, Florida, November 4–7.

Rader, Emilee. 2009. "Yours, Mine and (Not) Ours: Social Influences on Group Information Repositories." In *Proceedings of the SIGCHI Conference on Human Factors in Computing Systems*, 2095–2098. New York: ACM Press.

Raskin, Jef. 2000. *The Humane Interface: New Directions for Designing Interactive Systems*. New York: ACM Press/Addison-Wesley Publishing Co.

Ravasio, Pamela, Ljiljana Vukelja, Gabrio Rivera, and Moira C. Norrie. 2003. "Project InfoSpace: From Information Managing to Information Representation." In *Proceedings of INTERACT 2003*, edited by M. Rauterberg, M. Menozzi, and J. Wesson, 864–867. Amsterdam: IOS Press.

Ringel, M., E. Cutrell, S. Dumais, and E. Horvitz. 2003. "Milestones in Time: The Value of Landmarks in Retrieving Information from Personal Stores." In *Proceedings of INTERACT 2003*, edited by M. Rauterberg, M. Menozzi, and J. Wesson, 184–191. Amsterdam: IOS Press.

Robbins, Daniel C. 2008. "TapGlance: Designing a Unified Smartphone Interface for Personal Information Management." In *CHI 2009 Conference on Human Factors and Computing Systems*, 386–394. New York: ACM Press.

Rodden, Kerry, and Michael Leggett. 2010. "Best of Both Worlds: Improving Gmail Labels with the Affordances of Folders." In *Proceedings of the 28th International Conference Extended Abstracts on Human Factors in Computing Systems*, 4587–4596. New York: ACM Press.

Rodden, Kerry, and Kenneth R. Wood. 2003. "How Do People Manage Their Digital Photographs?" In *Proceedings of the SIGCHI Conference on Human Factors in Computing Systems*, 409–416. New York: ACM Press.

Rosch, Eleanor. 1978. "Principles of Categorization." In *Cognition and Categorization*, edited by E. Rosch and B. B. Lloyd, 27–48. Hillsdale, NJ: Erlbaum.

Rosch, Eleanor, Carolyn B. Mervis, Wayne D. Gray, David M. Johnson, and Penny Boyes-Braem. 1976. "Basic Objects in Natural Categories." *Cognitive Psychology* 8 (3): 382–439.

Rothenberg, Jeff. 1995. "Ensuring the Longevity of Digital Documents." *Scientific American* 272 (1): 42–47.

Russell, D., and S. Lawrence. 2007. "Search Everything." In *Personal Information Management*, edited by William Jones and Jaime Teevan, 153–166. Seattle: University of Washington Press.

Sajedi, Ali, Seyyed Hamidreza Afzali, and Zahra Zabardast. 2012. "Can You Retrieve a File on the Computer in Your First Attempt? Think to a New File Manager for Multiple Categorization of Your Personal Information." Paper presented at PIM12 CSCW 2012 Workshop, Seattle, Washington, February 11–15.

Saracevic, Tefko. 1999. "Information Science." *Journal of the American Society for Information Science* 50 (12): 1051–1063.

Sarvas, Risto, and David M. Frohlich. 2011. *From Snapshots to Social Media: The Changing Picture of Domestic Photography*. New York: Springer Science & Business Media.

Sauermann, Leo, Gunnar Grimnes, Malte Kiesel, Christiaan Fluit, Heiko Maus, Dominik Heim, Danish Nadeem, Benjamin Horak, and Andreas Dengel. 2006. "Semantic Desktop 2.0: The Gnowsis Experience." In *The Semantic Web—ISWC 2006*, 887–900. Berlin: Springer.

Schacter, Daniel L. 2008. *Searching for Memory: The Brain, the Mind, and the Past*. New York: Basic Books.

Schamber, Linda. 1994. "Relevance and Information Behavior." *Annual Review of Information Science and Technology* 29:3–48.

Sellen, Abigail J., and Richard H. R. Harper. *The Myth of the Paperless Office*. Cambridge, MA: MIT Press, 2002.

Sellen, Abigail, G. Louie, J. E. Harris, and A. J. Wilkins. 1997. "What Brings Intentions to Mind? An In Situ Study of Prospective Memory." *Memory* 5 (4): 483–507.

Sellen, Abigail, and Steve Whittaker. 2010. "Beyond Total Capture: A Constructive Critique of Lifelogging." *Communications of the ACM* 53 (5): 70–77.

Shami, N. Sadat, Michael Muller, and David Millen. 2011. "Browse and Discover: Social File Sharing in the Enterprise." In *Proceedings of the ACM 2011 Conference on Computer Supported Cooperative Work*, 295–304. New York: ACM Press.

Shneiderman, Ben. 1982. "The Future of Interactive Systems and the Emergence of Direct Manipulation." *Behaviour and Information Technology* 1 (3): 237–256.

Shneiderman, Ben, and C. Plaisant. 2010. *Designing the User Interface: Strategies for Effective Human–Computer Interaction*. 5th ed. Reading, MA: Addison-Wesley Co.

Tang, John C., Eric Wilcox, Julian A. Cerruti, Hernan Badenes, Stefan Nusser, and Jerald Schoudt. 2008. "Tag-It, Snag-It, or Bag-It: Combining Tags, Threads, and Folders in E-Mail." In *CHI '08 Conference on Human Factors in Computing Systems*, 2179–2194. New York: ACM Press.

Tauscher, Linda, and Saul Greenberg. 1997. "How People Revisit Web Pages: Empirical Findings and Implications for the Design of History Systems." *International Journal of Human–Computer Studies* 47 (1): 97–137. doi:10.1006/ijhc.1997.0125.

Taylor, Robert S. 1986. *Value Added Processes in Information Systems*. Edited by Melvin J. Voigt. Norwood, NJ: Ablex Publishing.

Teevan, Jaime, Christine Alvarado, Mark S. Ackerman, and David R. Karger. 2004. "The Perfect Search Engine Is Not Enough: A Study of Orienteering Behavior in Directed Search." In *SIGCHI Conference on Human Factors in Computing Systems*, edited by Elizabeth Dykstra-Erickson and Manfred Tscheligi, 415–422. New York: ACM Press.

Treisman, Anne M. 1969. "Strategies and Models of Selective Attention." *Psychological Review* 76 (3): 282.

Treisman, Anne M., and G. Gelade. 1980. "A Feature-Integration Theory of Attention." *Cognitive Psychology* 12:97–136.

Tulving, E., and D. M. Thomson. 1973. "Encoding Specificity and Retrieval Processes in Episodic Memory." *Psychological Review* 80:342–373.

Twomey, Fosnot Catherine, and Dolk Maarten. 1996. *Constructivism: Theory, Perspectives, and Practice*. New York: Teachers College Press.

Venolia, Gina Danielle, Laura Dabbish, J. J. Cadiz, and Anoop Gupta. 2001. "Supporting Email Workflow." Technical Report MSR-TR-2001-88, Microsoft Research, http://research.microsoft.com/apps/pubs/default.aspx?id=69881.

Venolia, Gina Danielle, and Carman Neustaedter. 2003. "Understanding Sequence and Reply Relationships within Email Conversations: A Mixed-Model Visualization." In *Proceedings of the SIGCHI Conference on Human Factors in Computing Systems*, 361–368. New York: ACM Press.

Voida, Amy, Judith S. Olson, and Gary M. Olson. 2013. "Turbulence in the Clouds: Challenges of Cloud-Based Information Work." In *CHI 2013 Conference on Human Factors in Computing Systems*, 2273–2282. New York: ACM Press.

Voida, Stephen, W. Keith Edwards, Mark W. Newman, Rebecca E. Grinter, and Nicolas Ducheneaut. 2006. "Share and Share Alike: Exploring the User Interface Affordances of File Sharing." In *Proceedings of the SIGCHI Conference on Human Factors in Computing Systems*, 221–230. New York: ACM Press.

Voit, Karl, Keith Andrews, and Wolfgang Slany. 2012. "Tagging Might Not Be Slower than Filing in Folders." In *Proceedings of the 2012 ACM Annual Conference Extended Abstracts on Human Factors in Computing Systems Extended Abstracts*, 2063–2068. New York: ACM Press.

Wagenaar, Willem A. 1986. "My Memory: A Study of Autobiographical Memory over Six Years." *Cognitive Psychology* 18 (2): 225–252.

Wagenaar, Willem A. 1994. "Is Memory Self-Serving?" In *The Remembering Self: Construction and Accuracy in the Self-Narrative*, edited by U. Neisser and R. Fivush, 191–204. Cambridge: Cambridge University Press.

Wash, R., and E. Radar. 2007. "Public Bookmarks and Private Benefits: An Analysis of Incentives in Social Computing." *Proceedings of the American Society for Information Science and Technology* 44 (1): 1–13. doi:10.1002/meet.1450440240.

Wen, James. 2003. "Post-Valued Recall Web Pages: User Disorientation Hits the Big Time." *IT and Society* 1 (3): 184–194.

Whittaker, Steve. 1996. "Talking to Strangers: An Evaluation of the Factors Affecting Electronic Collaboration." In *Proceedings of the 1996 ACM Conference on Computer Supported Cooperative Work*, 409–418. New York: ACM Press.

Whittaker, Steve. 2005. "Supporting Collaborative Task Management in Email." *Human–Computer Interaction* 20:49–88.

Whittaker, Steve. 2011. "Personal Information Management: From Information Consumption to Curation." *Annual Review of Information Science and Technology* 45:3–62.

Whittaker, Steve, Victoria Bellotti, and Jacek Gwizdka. 2007. "Everything through Email." In *Personal Information Management*, edited by William Jones and Jaime Teevan, 167–189. Seattle: University of Washington Press.

Whittaker, Steve, Ofer Bergman, and Paul Clough. 2010. "Easy on That Trigger Dad: A Study of Long Term Family Photo Retrieval." *Personal and Ubiquitous Computing* 14 (1): 31–43.

Whittaker, Steve, and Julia Hirschberg. 2001. "The Character, Value, and Management of Personal Paper Archives." *ACM Transactions on Computer–Human Interaction* 8 (2): 150–170. doi: 10.1145/376929.376932.

Whittaker, Steve, Julia Hirschberg, Brian Amento, Litza Stark, Michiel Bacchiani, Philip Isenhour, Larry Stead, Gary Zamchick, and Aaron Rosenberg. 2002. "SCANMail: A Voicemail Interface That Makes Speech Browsable, Readable and Searchable." In *Proceedings of the SIGCHI Conference on Human Factors in Computing Systems*, 275–282. New York: ACM Press.

Whittaker, Steve, Quentin Jones, Bonnie Nardi, Mike Creech, Loren Terveen, Ellen Isaacs, and John Hainsworth. 2004. "ContactMap: Organizing Communication in a Social Desktop." *ACM Transactions on Computer–Human Interaction* 11 (4): 445–471.

Whittaker, Steve, Patrick Hyland, and Myrtle Wiley. 1994. "FILOCHAT: Handwritten Notes Provide Access to Recorded Conversations." In *Proceedings of the SIGCHI Conference on Human Factors in Computing Systems: Celebrating Interdependence*, 271–277. New York: ACM Press.

Whittaker, Steve, Quentin Jones, and Loren Terveen. 2002. "Contact Management: Identifying Contacts to Support Long-Term Communication." In *Proceedings of the 2002 ACM Conference on Computer Supported Cooperative Work*, 216–225. New York: ACM Press.

Whittaker, Steve, Vaiva Kalnikaité, Daniela Petrelli, Abigail Sellen, Nicolas Villar, Ofer Bergman, Paul Clough, and Jens Brockmeier. 2012. "Socio-Technical Lifelogging: Deriving Design Principles for a Future Proof Digital Past." *Human–Computer Interaction* 27 (1–2): 37–62.

Whittaker, Steve, Tara Matthews, Julian Cerruti, Hernan Badenes, and John Tang. 2011. "Am I Wasting My Time Organizing Email? A Study of Email Refinding." In *Proceedings of the SIGCHI Conference on Human Factors in Computing Systems*, 3449–3458). New York: ACM Press.

Whittaker, Steve, and Candace Sidner. 1996. "Email Overload: Exploring Personal Information Management of Email." In *Proceedings of the SIGCHI Conference on Human Factors in Computing Systems: Common Ground*, 276–283. New York: ACM Press.

Whittaker, Steve, Jerry Swanson, Jakov Kucan, and Candy Sidner. 1997. "TeleNotes: Managing Lightweight Interactions in the Desktop." *ACM Transactions on Computer–Human Interaction* 4 (2): 137–168.

Whittaker, Steve, Simon Tucker, Kumutha Swampillai, and Rachel Laban. 2008. "Design and Evaluation of Systems to Support Interaction Capture and Retrieval." *Personal and Ubiquitous Computing* 12 (3): 197–221.

Wilhelm, Anita, Yuri Takhteyev, Risto Sarvas, Nancy Van House, and Marc Davis. 2004. "Photo Annotation on a Camera Phone." In *CHI '04 Extended Abstracts on Human Factors in Computing Systems*, 1403–1406. New York: ACM Press.

Wilson, Tom D. 1981. "On User Studies and Information Needs." *Journal of Documentation* 37 (1): 3–15.

Wilson, Tom D. 1994. "Information Needs and Uses: Fifty Years of Progress?" In *Fifty Years of Information Progress: A Journal of Documentation Review*, ed. B. C. Vickory, 15–51. London: Aslib.

Wilson, Tom D. 1999. "Models in Information Behaviour Research." *Journal of Documentation* 55 (3): 249–270.

Woerndl, Wolfgang, and Maximilian Woehrl. 2008. "SeMoDesk: Towards a Mobile Semantic Desktop." Paper presented at Proceedings Personal Information Management (PIM) Workshop, CHI '08 conference, Florence, Italy, April 5–10.

Yarosh, Svetlana, Tara Matthews, Thomas P. Moran, and Barton Smith. 2009. "What Is an Activity? Appropriating an Activity-Centric System." In *Human–Computer Interaction—INTERACT 2009*, 582–595. Berlin: Springer.

Index